BRAVE EUROPE?

The Origins of the EU from Paris in 1870 to Berlin in 1942 to Strasbourg in 1944 to Brussels in 1957 to Berlin in 1964

Mick Greenhough

Shield Crest

© Copyright 2017   Mick Greenhough

All rights reserved

ISBN: 978-1-911090-48-9

MMXVII

A CIP catalogue record for this book is available from the British Library

Published by
ShieldCrest Publishing Ltd.,
Aylesbury, Buckinghamshire,
HP22 5RR   England
Tel: +44 (0) 333 8000 890
www.shieldcrest.co.uk

THE AUTHOR

Married with a son, Mick Greenhough came from a coal mining family in Derbyshire and has lived in Kent for 65 years.

He is a chartered Mechanical Engineer and has travelled extensively advising on underwater construction in UK and several overseas countries including; Poland, France, Cyprus and Hong Kong among others.

He is a member of the National Union of Journalists and has been a committee member of the London branch. He has written for Lloyds Register Marine div (now LHS) and is currently working with Queen Mary's University, London on Tidal Flow Power.

As a committee member of the Campaign for an Independent Britain he has stood for election as an MP. Passionate about the future of Britain he decided to put pen to paper to release his findings following extensive research into the origins of the EU. The result is 'Brave New Europe'.

CONTENTS

INTRODUCTION

The UK has had a Referendum whether to leave the EU or Remain. The country voted to leave by a considerable majority. Its significance can be compared to a combination of the evacuation of Dunkerque and The Battle of Britain.

However it would seem that the majority of those who voted to remain in the EU and those who voted to leave were not fully aware of what they were voting for or against.

Many Brexiteers voted primarily for control of immigration and with a gut feeling that there was something particularly rotten and undemocratic about the EU.

The Remainers, particularly Generation Snowflake,[1] generally believe it to be merely a trading bloc, reducing mobile roaming charges and a way to keep peace in Europe. This is due to the lopsided education they have been fed by the BBC, mainstream media, schools and universities of what the EU is about.

But what about the 100 or so MPs who are rejecting the democratic vote and plotting to block Brexit?

The Brexiteers exaggerated somewhat while the performance of the Remainers, Main Stream Media and BBC was particularly disgraceful.

Unsubstantiated and overblown speculation was presented as known certainties to the point of farce with Project Fear. The BBC continually giving out subliminal pro EU messages and their interviewers blatantly biased in favour of Remain. Their self-acclaimed reputation for even-handedness has, yet again, been seriously compromised.

---

[1] "Generation Snowflake" refers to young people, typically university or college students, who react with distress to the expression of ideas that they believe to be offensive or emotionally challenging. Usually white and had a soft upbringing by doting middle class parents.

This book is to present the origins of the EU and its remit for the reader to draw their own conclusions and whether their vote for the Referendum was the right one. It contains much information in the public domain that is scattered, hidden and generally ignored by the Main Stream Media.

It is also for you to decide is if the EU is a malign form of government and if supporting the UK being in it can define you as a Quisling[2].

Much is said about the Single Market. It is a sweet name to disguise its real nature.

The Single Market is not a version of Pettycoat Lane writ large as Remainers like to promote. It is not really a market at all – it's a Single Regulatory Regime that comes with several sneaky political 'add ons' to ensure the EU remains in control.

- Uncontrolled migration from EU into UK
- submission to the primacy of the European Court of Justice (The remit of the EJC is not for justice but to make judgements that further 'ever closer union')
- Accept the supremacy of EU law over English Common Law
- Acceptance of all EU standards even when not applicable to UK.

These are euphemistically called the 'Four Freedoms' by the EU. They are in fact chains to bind a country into permanent subservience to the EU.

Soft Brexit is a euphemism for Hard Remain.

---

[2] Vidkun Quisling was a Norwegian politician who betrayed his country to a malign foreign power – the Nazis. His name has gone down in history as the epithet for any such politician. The 100 MPs in parliament are plotting to thwart Brexit and betray UK a malign foreign power also – the EU. Does then the epithet of 'Quisling' therefore suit them . After reading this book make up your own minds.

For many years I was completely unaware of the significance of the EU. When I began to find out more about it, the more I discovered the more appalled I became at the betrayal of the people of our country by those who can only be described as 'Quisling Politicians'. The mainstream media, and especially the BBC, kept a sinister silence. I therefore believe that all the citizens of UK should be fully aware of the information which is now contained within this book.

Some 9 years ago I produced a small successful booklet entitled 'Brave New Europe?' and this is an updated and more comprehensive version. I have collated and written information into what I hope is a reasonably uncomplicated read. The relevant documents and quotes located in an appendix to which the reader can refer.

*N.B. In the appendix you are able to refer to the original document where the article appeared which is more comprehensive. To get to the original document it is necessary to visit **www.theeuroprobe.org** and simply type BNE the search box and scroll down. **Each reference cited in the book is the number on the list of posts under that heading**. If you wish to comment on posts, go to Ref 47. "Brexit has won the battle but not yet the war as we are still in the EU" (Appendix 45).Electronic versions of this book will have active hyperlinks*

The main stream media and especially the BBC try to suppress or ignore this information and Europhiles try to dismiss it as of no consequence. The evidence, however, is overwhelming and presented for you to make up your own mind.

The book was started before the referendum and completed after the result was known so the timing of some comments within must be read with this in mind.

Quote from the booklet sent to everyone prior to the vote on June 23rd 2016 to vote to leave or remain in the EU.

A once in a generation decision

The referendum on Thursday, 23rd June is your chance to decide if we should remain in or leave the European Union.

The Government believes it is in the best interests of the UK to remain in the EU.

This is the way to protect jobs, provide security, and strengthen the UK's economy for every family in this country – a clear path into the future, in contrast to the uncertainty of leaving.

This is your decision. The Government will implement what you decide.

If you're aged 18 or over by 23rd June and are entitled to vote, this is your chance to decide.

Registration ends on 7th June. Find out how to register at *Aboutmyvote.co.uk* and register online at *Gov.uk/register-to-vote*

If you would like to know more about any of the information in this leaflet, go to: *EUReferendum.gov.uk*

Despite massive pro EU propaganda from the Government, using taxpayers' money, the BBC, using licence payers' money, and many institutions using EU funding the decision of the voters was to leave the EU. No Ifs, no buts, no mention of second referendum or allowing Quisling MPs the opportunity to frustrate Brexit.

The EU's Modus Operandi is secrecy, deceit and lying.

- Jean-Claude Juncker, President of the European Commission: *"When it becomes serious, you have to lie" (Appendix 48)*
- Ted Heath, when UK PM : *"I had to lie to parliament and the people to get the 1972 Act voted through as the British public are too stupid to govern themselves"* (Appendix 65)
- A British minister responsible for open government ruled that exchange rate parities the ERM (European Exchange Rate Mechanism) and EMU (European Monetary Union) were subjects about which the government could legitimately lie to Parliament. (*Bernard Connolly – Appendix 3*)

- How the EU funds institutions to ensure they 'stay on message'.

> I'VE just mugged a 'Remain' supporter — I took £350 out of his wallet, but he didn't seem to mind.
> I felt a bit sorry for him, so I gave half of it back, but only on the condition that he spent it on things I say he can and that everything he buys should have a picture next to it of me saying I'd paid for it. He agreed!
> We are meeting again tomorrow to do the same thing. He said that it was a fantastic idea and that he wouldn't be able to survive without me.
> *DIANE SANSON, Northwich, Cheshire.*

Many University professors think this is a superb way to get science funding. It goes to show that intelligence and common sense do not necessarily go together. QED *(Appendix 48)*

The European Union

It is important to be aware that the EU was set up from the start to be a completely undemocratic organisation. From then on has been developing into a Frankenstein Union and heading for a police state *(Appendix 6])*. It is maintained by a bureaucracy (the *Nomenklatura*) heavily bribed with high salaries and pensions to stay 'on message'.

The concept of the EU is that it will be 'supra national'. That is, Europe will be governed by an undemocratically appointed elite administration *'above the control of national elected politicians and the enfranchised voters'* for the 'common good'. By the 'common good' it means the exclusive good of the elite administration and their acolytes – certainly not that of the lumpen citizenry.

For this to work, the best interests of the member nations and their peoples have to be subjugated to the best interests of the elite administration and academics. The elite would no longer have any loyalty or accountability to their nation and peoples.

Several people thought of other similar 'EU' ways of running Europe but it is the most sinister option that has become today's EU. Although the aims of the Europhiles and the Nazis were not entirely the same they are broadly similar in that they were/are arrogant control freaks with complete contempt for democracy and the citizens.

There have been four major attempts to have a single European state. The Roman Empire, Charlemagne's Holy Roman Empire, Napoleon's First French Empire and Hitler's Third Reich. All four were based on various forms of slavery or feudalism. All four operated utterly undemocratically with brutal suppression of any opposition. Eventually all four failed catastrophically.

However such 'order' as they envisaged can only be achieved at the expense of freedom of the individual and free speech.

The EU is the latest venture and is the essentially the same model of undemocratic rule by an unelected elite.

See Appendix 7 for books that are must-reads if you want to know the full extent to which the citizens of the UK have been betrayed by our political elite

The Nazi project was killed off in 1945, or so we thought, but it has been reborn in conjunction with the Frankfurt School of Marxism as the European Union Project.

In a crass and ill-timed intervention, the unelected president of the European Council Herman Van Rompuy has warned Vladimir Putin that the EU intends ultimately to control every country on the western flank of Russia. *(Appendix 64)*

Is the EU a fascist body? *(See appendix 6)*

≈1≈

The Beginning

B efore 1870 Northern Europe was a patchwork of small independent states. In 1870 a loose confederation of German speaking dukedoms and statelets came together under the leadership of Prussia to invade France and occupy Paris. In 1871 they formally united to establish a new state of Germany.

By 1900 this new Germany with its inventive and vigorous work ethic had developed both industrially and commercially to become a very successful and powerful presence in Europe, rivalling France and Great Britain.

The new German political elite became very envious of the British Empire and, to a lesser extent, the Dutch, French and Portuguese Empires. It is important to understand that the British Empire was essentially a Trading Empire for the export of the products of the booming industrial revolution rather than an Empire of conquest. Little attempt was made to 'rule and impose' or enforce our culture except almost by default and where lands were considered 'empty' they were settled.

Military force was used where our Trade Lines and trading were threatened and to 'persuade' reluctant countries to allow Britain to trade with them. Germany began energetically to try and carve out their own empire but Britain, France and the Dutch had, by then, acquired all the lucrative parts of the world.

Because of their developing power compared to the rest of Europe some of the German political elite began to believe they should be 'the chosen ones' to bring 'order' to the whole of Europe. However such 'order' as they envisaged could only be achieved at the expense of freedom of the individual and free speech.

In 1914 the First World War began, almost by accident, although many were spoiling for a fight anyway. The assassination of Franz Ferdinand, the Archduke of Austria-Este and the heir to Austro-Hungarian throne was not the cause but it was the hair trigger that fired the starting gun.

However Germany saw it as an opportunity to grab control of the French and Dutch Empires if they won. When Britain became involved they hoped to acquire much of the British Empire as well.

The German Chancellor's private secretary, Kurt Riezler, drafted the *September programme*[3] on 9 September 1914, in the early days of the German attack in the west. Germany expected to defeat France as quickly and decisively as they had done in 1870. They proposed a united Europe controlled by Germany and run from Berlin when they thought they had won in autumn 1914. This looks like the first inklings of a similar idea to the modern European Union except that the *Septemberprogramm* did not envisage Britain as a subject province.

Germany lost the war and its people were left with an exaggerated sense of grievance, believing they had been betrayed. They felt they had lost mainly because of the blockade by the Royal Navy rather than on the battlefield. Indeed the German army was allowed to march home in good military order with all their arms and equipment. The blockade had reduced the German population to near starvation.

The appalling behaviour of the French occupying force after the war contributed considerably to German anger. They lost faith in the political state and as a result a revolutionary fervour swept Germany.

---

[3] The Septemberprogramm was the plan for the territorial expansion of Imperial Germany, prepared for Chancellor Theobald von Bethmann-Hollweg, at the beginning of World War I (1914–18).

One event during that war was to have a traumatic effect on the psyches of both France and Germany. That was the battle of Verdun where a deliberate decision was made by the leaders for the two armies to fight and win the battle by absolute attrition i.e. to 'bleed the French army white'. The politicians and generals poured soldiers into the battle, the idea of winning was having the last soldier standing regardless of the casualties.

The battle of the Somme was fought by the British army, against the advice of Haig, as the French insisted they desperately needed a diversion to draw German soldiers away from Verdun. The casualties in these two battles on all sides was truly horrendous – over 1 million men. However the French and German losses were by far the greater.

Post war this led to a desire that such industrialised slaughter should never be allowed to happen again. It also led to the notion that the soldiers' courage in the fight against 'the enemy' was the result of the pride people have in their national roots.[4] This then led to a new political philosophy: that the nationalities of Europe should be destroyed by mixing them all up to become a single homogeneous, undifferentiated people. This is now known as the Coudenhove–Kalergi Plan – The Pan European Movement *(Appendix 4)*.

In the aftermath of the war Germany was in turmoil. Quantitative Easing destroyed the value of money, (the *'Reichsmark'* was introduced in 1924 as a permanent replacement for the Papiermark,) reducing the German public to extreme poverty. Rival political groups fought savage street battles for control.

---

[4] *Soldiers would never choose to have a battle of absolute attrition; they do what they are ordered to do. The motivation comes from the arrogance and greed of the military and political elite.*

In 1917 Lenin and his Bolsheviks, with considerable help from Germany, hijacked the Russian revolution and enforced Lenin's form of Marxism.

During the 1920s several 'United Europe' ideas began to take shape: Frankfurt School, National Socialism, Pan European Movement, EU and the New World Order.

A number of German Intellectuals and Academics around the Institute for Social Research, particularly in universities of Frankfurt am Main, became very enamoured with the Leninist version of Marxism. This was where the society was run by self-selected intellectuals, academics and professional politicians with the common people excluded completely. The ruling of the undemocratic Europe was to be the exclusive function of the unelected political elite.

They later became known as the Frankfurt School of Marxism. Their desire was for a Soviet Germany to control all Europe and become similar to the Russian Soviet State run, of course, by themselves. Brutal suppression of all opposition would be necessary for them to maintain their control. The voting citizens were to be nothing more than ballot fodder. *(Chapter 2 and appendix 3)*.

However Hitler (himself a Socialist) beat them to that prize so they all ran away to the universities of USA and UK. Hitler then promoted the concept of 'The Master Race' to a lunatic degree. He wanted a 'pure' Aryan population (although Aryan is a language group, not a race,) whereas the Coudenhove Pan European Movement wanted a population all mixed together – except for the ruling elite.

In 1933 Hitler brought in the Enabling Act that was essentially the model for the later EU Lisbon Treaty.

The Enabling Act allowed the Nazi Cabinet to introduce legislation without it first going through the Reichstag. Any legislation passed by the Cabinet did not need presidential approval either.*(Appendix 3)*

All previous legislation could be revoked at will without consulting the elected Reichstag. The Act had a lifespan of four years before it had to be renewed via the Reichstag – something that happened on two separate occasions with an even more Nazified Reichstag and with what was effectively open voting.

In the 1920s the seeds of the concept of a parallel federal supranational Europe began to be promoted by Monnet. Based on the ideas of English diplomat Arthur Salter. This was quite unconnected with the Nazi movement. However its concept was very similar in that it was to be completely undemocratic.

It was not just in Europe that the desire for state control was becoming fashionable. In the UK radio was rapidly developing causing alarm within the UK Establishment and in 1922 the BBC was formed to control all information distributed by radio *(Appendix 38).*

There was a third movement. In 1922 a rather shadowy character, Richard Coudenhove-Kalergi, founded the "Pan-European" movement in Vienna, which aimed to create a New World Order in Europe *(Appendix 4)* by deliberately mixing and cross breeding all the tribes of the individual nations with migrants from Africa and Asia to form a homogeneous population.

The white races of Europe should be destroyed and replaced with a race of Eurasian-Negroids who can be easily controlled by the ruling elite.

Judeophile and EU 'founding father' Richard Coudenhove-Kalergi in 'Praktischer Idealismus' 1924

Then onto the world population.

This seems to be being implemented by the EU with mass migration to achieve what they call 'ethnic dilution'.

The Pan European 'Flag' they devised is shown. The similarity with the EU 'flag' is clear. They are not 'flags' however as only states have flags - more accurately called 'banners'. *(Appendix 11).*

When the infamous Marxist Eric Hobsbawn was asked if Stalin's mass murder of 20 million was worth it to achieve a Russian Socialist state he replied 'Of course'.

Today the EU could equally say 'The mass rapes of white European women are acceptable if it helps to destroy European cultures to achieve a Socialist European State?'

In 1938 a group of German bureaucrats began to develop their own ideas with a draft document on how Europe should be governed.

By 1942 they were confident that they were about to win the European War. They held a conference in Berlin on how they were going to rule Europe after the final victory. The name of this meeting was *Europaische Wirtschafts Gemeinsschaft* (EWG), the European Economic Community or EEC. This was destined to become used as the first draft of the European Union in 1964. *(See translation at appendix 9).*

The meeting was chaired by Walter Funk and hovering in the background was a Walter Hallstein.

Though not a member of the Nazi party, Hallstein was an active member of the Nazi leadership programme and a supporter of the 'Blood and Honour' philosophy and 'Nuremburg Race laws'.[5]

Within this draft was the aim to de-industrialize the UK and reduce it to serfdom. Essentially what the EU has been doing. *(Appendix 10).*

These two concepts followed independent but parallel courses until the Nazi option ended abruptly in 1945.

Each year the EU award the Charlemagne prize to the politician or Bureaucrat who has made a major contribution to *ever closer union* and the Coudenhove Plan *(Appendix 4).*

We also have the curious 1995 Barcelona Treaty between the EU and the African states of the southern Mediterranean rim. Not much is said about it but seems to have has within its remit to eventually form a new state of Eurabia. This would allow all the countries of N Africa free and unfettered access to Europe. It is a French/Arab initiative to counteract US domination. It originated with De Gaulle who was distraught at the loss of Algeria and the dominance of the USA. Whether it is just a cooperative Treaty between Europe and Arabia to ease tensions or rather more is something about which the reader must make up their own mind. The treaty is claimed to be a precursor for the new state of Eurabia and to consolidate the EU Coudenhove plan. *(Appendix 61).*

The post war plan

The 1942 German EWG envisaged that England was to be completely dismantled and divided up into 9 Regions (each run by a Gauleiter). It was to be de-industrialised, all the manufacturing and science based activity transferred to Germany. The UK was to become a giant feudal slave state to provide food for the Third Reich.

---

[5] *There is more of Walter Hallstein later as he was to become the first EU president. Less than 10% of Germans were members of the Nazi party*

In 1944 the Nazis held another conference in Strasbourg. It was clear by then that Germany was going to lose the war. This conference was to decide how Germany could win the peace *(Appendix 12)*. SS Obergruppenfuhrer Dr Scheid led the meeting to establish what was to eventually become the EU. Whether it was his original thought or he knew of Monnet's ideas is not known but it came into being in 1964.

After the war much of Germany was devastated. Konrad Adenauer became Chancellor of Germany. He was a devout Catholic and made it his job to rebuild Germany but he clearly had a latent desire for Germany to eventually rule Europe.

The Vichy French and bureaucrats in other European countries occupied by the Nazis had also had a taste of non-accountable authority and they rather liked it. They quite admired Nazi rule but when Germany lost they quickly moved over to the Frankfurt School as they were now deemed the winners. They just changed hats, but sat at the same desks and carried on as before: most wartime Vichy French and German bureaucrats remained in office after the war.

The De-Nazification programme had to be halted due to the military threat from Russia.

Francois Mitterrand was one who actively worked for, and supported, the Vichy government until it looked as if Germany would lose the war. He later became a fervent EU supporter and also the president of France. He told his close confident, Magoudi, *"I will take my revenge on the English upstarts. I will destroy their beloved island by linking it with Europe."*

In 1945 the German Reich hit the buffers leaving the way open for Monnet's option as an alternative federal Europe but the 1944 German 'EU' was to win out.

In the late 1940s the Marxists of the Frankfurt School and several other European Marxists and European socialists (Monnet, Paul-Henri Spaak and Altiero Spinelli) began to plan the EU. Their scheme did not become the EU we have now, however they very much liked what did come to be.

Some of the very senior Nazi bureaucrats, eg Hans Blobke, Walter Funk and Walter Hallstein, were involved in the production of the 1938 and 1942 EWG documents. Some also became committee members or closely involved with the 1942 committee, later on the Coal & Steel committee, then on to the proto-EU committee *(Appendix 12)*.

All 5 German members of the 1964 committee planning to hijack the EU had been active members of the IG Farben/Nazi coalition during WWII[6]. *(Appendix 59)*

Coal & Steel are the fuel of military ambitions and so Coal and Steel production was taken out of national control and put under supranational control.

Hallstein was a political butterfly dabbling in Nazi organisations; while never in the Nazi party he was very close to the leaders. However, he was an enthusiastic member of the Nazi Leadership project and supporter of the 'Nuremberg Racial Laws' and the 'Blood and Honour' Nazi philosophy that led to the Holocaust, and the notion of a Greater Germany. He survived the war without injury or retribution and never atoned for his quasi-Nazi past

---

[6] *The IG Farben/Nazi-coalition was responsible for the deaths of 60 million people and the destruction of half of Europe during WWII. This would be their third attempt to conquer Europe. It would not take place in military uniforms but in the grey suits of the corporate and political stakeholders of the cartel.*

Less than 10 % 0f Germans were members of the Nazi Party but most went along with them when they were winning. If not they had a good chance of ending up in a Concentration camp.

≈2≈

The Frankfurt School of Marxism

The Frankfurt School university lecturers in the US and UK universities have been able to manipulate and influence the naive and impressionable mind-set of hundreds of their students and fellow academics. The consequence of this lop sided education is Generation Snowflake. Many of those students are now in significant positions of control in our institutions *(Appendix 8)*. Among others they affect the Foreign and Commonwealth Office, the Treasury, the police, the law, and in particular the BBC, police and the education establishment. Many in these institutions may well be unaware that they are implementing Frankfurt School philosophy. It is the philosophy promoted by Common Purpose *(Appendix 2)*. See also The Cult Of Alinsky and how the US Democratic Party was Hijacked *(Appendix 8)*.

The Frankfurt School is steadily furthering its 'quiet' cultural revolution, while giving us no idea about their plans for the future. It is to ultimately destroy our democratic culture, individual freedoms, family life and the individual cultures of the various European countries. They are to be replaced with a single 'European culture' within a Soviet style state run by the Frankfurt School/Leninist elite.
Their big chance came with the Vietnam War, the chaos on campuses and Flower Power.

It became known as the Age of Aquarius and of Liberated Personal Freedom (in reality the covert Frankfurt School of Marxism was beginning to have an effect). *(Appendix 3)*

While it has no 'Mr Big' or Bible/Koran/Mein Kampf it is a philosophy that many intellectuals and politicians find very attractive indeed. It gives them unelected authority and unaccountability, secure jobs, good salaries and pensions with an exaggerated sense of their own importance. Good for their egos. They can then order the disenfranchised citizens about without sanction.

To achieve this end the Frankfurt School of Marxism promotes:

- 1. The creation of racism offences and to promote the view that pride in one's nation is equal to hatred of other nations and peoples.

- 2. Continual change to create confusion

- 3.The teaching of sex and homosexuality to very young children

- 4.The undermining of discipline in schools and teachers' authority

- 5. Mass immigration into UK and Europe to destroy national identities. (**see below) by ethnic dilution.

- 6. The promotion of excessive drinking and drugs.

- 7. Emptying of Christian churches, especially the Protestant churches who have strong democratic traditions.*** and promoting rival religions.

- 8. An unreliable legal system where criminals have the same rights as the victim. The victim is considered as guilty as the criminal but with a bias always against victims of crime.

- 9. Dependency on the state or state benefits.

- 10. Control and dumbing down of media and education.

- 11. Encouraging the breakdown of family life by funding fatherless families to the detriment of married parents. ("To achieve One World Government it is necessary to remove from the minds of men their individualism, their loyalty to family traditions and national identification." - **Brock Chisholm**, when director of the UN World Health Organisation. It should be remembered that the UN Charter was written Alger Hiss later exposed as a closet Marxist)

- 12. To keep the population in a constant state of fear and anxiety a string of phony crises are generated from Killer Eggs to Global Warming due to Man. This makes it much easier to convince people to give up many of their traditional freedoms to 'save the world'. The Club of Rome *(Appendix 13)*

- 13 Biased teaching against Christianity in schools. Protestant Christianity has an ethos of individualism and democratic principles. These are an anathema for Establishment control. *(Appendix 57)*

- 14. Schools to teach **British** pupils to be ashamed of their national and family history and have no self-respect for themselves.

- 15). Very many University academics now support this philosophy and it is difficult to get a University teaching post unless you do

- The Frankfurt School aim is destroy the separate national cultures of Europe to replace with a single Soviet style culture. To have a single homogeneous cattle-like population of Europe governed undemocratically by an obscenely wealthy Political Elite.

≈3≈

1943 – 1957

In 1944 the Germans realised they could not win the war. A meeting was held in Strasbourg to organise how to win the peace. The strategy they came up with was a bureaucratic and undemocratic society and they made preparations to set it up a post war to reassert its ambitions to rule Europe after the war *(Appendix 11)*. They would not use guns and tanks but business suits, bureaucratic procedures and the vast stocks of stolen money hidden outside of Germany.

In late 1944 during the last months of the war Germany transferred vast quantities of stolen money, confiscated or looted assets, jewellery, gold and wealth to 'safe havens' outside of Germany in preparation for their plan to win the peace.

The five other countries that formed the EEC were almost destitute after the war except Germany which had access to that enormous hidden wealth. Their coffers had been emptied by the Nazis during the war.

The Catholic Church was complicit in the escape of many of the worst Nazis to Argentina and South America. Of the 9,000 Nazis who escaped to South America after the war 5,000 went to Argentina. President Juan Peron issued thousands of blank passports used by the Nazi escape system called ODESSA to allow SS members to escape.

The main contact point and provider of help was the German Roman Catholic Bishop in Rome, Bishop Alois Hudal who worked with the full co-operation of the Austrian Office in Rome. German, Austrian, Croatian and Ukrainian Nazis were the predominant nationalities he helped to escape.

In 1945 the de-Nazification of Germany began. Communist East Germany was formed with a massive Soviet tank army stationed just east of the Iron Curtain. The increasing Soviet threat caused the US to stop the de-Nazification programme.

The USA then began to financially support the rebuilding of European industry. The Marshall Aid plan was to act as a buffer to the Soviet threat and provide markets for US industry greatly expanded for war production.

In the UK the Labour Government, advised by its resident economic socialist experts, freely chose not to make industrial modernisation the central theme in our use of Marshall Aid. They chose to politically use the money to nationalise industries still equipped with machine tools and equipment clapped out after six years of intensive war production.

Germany re-equipped their industry with new machine tools and equipment. They also had huge reserves of capital hidden overseas; Added to this, the British wartime bureaucracy had been very active in necessarily controlling society and industrial production. Post war it was very easy for them to continue controlling the newly nationalised industries. In devastated Germany they let their engineers and entrepreneurs rebuild without the heavy bureaucracy and their economy blossomed. This was the foundation and root of the 'German post war miracle' and their current industrial success and political strength, and the decline of our industries.

Konrad Adenauer refused to recognise East Germany and so many Nazi war criminals still in the West German

Civil Service and institutions were not sent east to account for their war crimes. They simply changed hats, sat at the same desks and carried on in the same jobs they had under the Nazis. Some of these were members of the Nazi/IG Farben-coalition who became members of the committee setting up the embryonic EU *(Appendix 12)*.

Hallstein was made the first president of the proto EU and he used the German 1942 document as the first draft. In 1944 they decided to use something similar to the EU to win the peace. Post war they helped initiate the proposed EU. It is not an exaggeration to call the EU the child of the Third Reich.

It is very easy for senior bureaucrats to swap ideologies to keep their jobs and perks as the political climate changes. It was almost as if the wartime Nazi fascists and the European Leninist Marxists came together for their own mutual benefit.

However, despite again losing the war, many of the German Elite still yearned to rule Europe.

Originally the US was also very keen on the EU as they thought it would be a means to stop Germany re-arming again, block the Soviet threat and rebuild Europe as a market for US goods.

It was the presence of the US army (as NATO) on the East German border and particularly the nuclear balance that kept the peace in Europe for 60 years. Certainly not the EU.

Quoting from "The Rising Beast: Germany in the Balkans" by Gerald Flurry *[Appendix 11]*.

US Military Intelligence report EW-Pa 128
Enclosure No. 1 to despatch No. 19,489 of Nov. 27, 1944, from the Embassy at London, England.

(http://www.ganino.com/contact#form-1)

SECRET

SUPREME HEADQUARTERS
ALLIED EXPEDITIONARY FORCE
Office of Assistant Chief of Staff, G-2
7 November 1944

INTELLIGENCE REPORT NO. EW-Pa 128

SUBJECT: Plans of German industrialists to engage in underground activity after Germany's defeat; flow of capital to neutral countries.

SOURCE: Agent of French Deuxieme Bureau, recommended by Commandant Zindel. This agent is regarded as reliable and has worked for the French on German problems since 1916. He was in close contact with the Germans, particularly industrialists, during the occupation of France and he visited Germany as late as August, 1944.

1. A meeting of the principal German industrialists with interests in France was held on August 10, 1944, in the Hotel Rotes Haus in Strasbourg, France, and attended by the informant indicated above as the source. Among those present were the following:

Dr. Scheid, who presided, holding the rank of S.S.
> Obergruppenfuhrer and Director of the Heche
> (Hermandorff & Schonburg) Company.

Dr. Kaspar, representing Krupp.

Dr. Tolle, representing Rochling.

Dr. Sinderen, representing Messerschmitt

Drs. Kopp, Vier and Beerwanger, representing Rheinmetall.

Captain Haberkorn and Dr. Ruhe, representing Bussing.

Drs. Ellenmayer and Kardos, representing Volkswagenwerk.

Engineers Drose, Yanchew and Koppshem, representing various factories in Posen, Poland (Drose, Yanchew and Co., Brown-Boveri, Herkuleswerke,

uschwerke, and Stadtwerke)

Captain Dornbuach, head of the Industrial Inspection Section at Posen.

Dr. Meyer, an official of the German Naval Ministry in Paris.

Dr. Strossner, of the Ministry of Armament, Paris.

2.   Dr. Scheid stated that all industrial materiel in France was to be evacuated to Germany immediately. The battle of France was lost for Germany and now the defence of the Siegfried Line was the main problem. From now on also German industry must realize that the war cannot be won and that it must take steps to prepare for a post-war commercial campaign. Each industrialist must make contacts and alliances with foreign firms, but this must be done individually and without attracting any suspicion. Moreover, the groundwork would have to be done at the financial level for borrowing considerable sums from foreign countries after the war.

As examples of the kind of penetration which had been most useful in the past, Dr. Scheid cited the fact that patents for stainless steel belonged to the Chemical Foundation, Inc., New York, and the Krupp company of Germany jointly and that the U.S. Steel Corporation, Carnegie Illinois, American Steel and Wire, and National Tube, etc. were thereby under an obligation to work with the Krupp concern. He also cited the Zeiss Company, the Leika Company and the Hamburg-American Line as firms which had been especially effective in protecting German interests abroad, and gave their New York addresses to the industrialists at this meeting.

3. Following this meeting a smaller one was held presided over by Dr. Bosse of the German Armaments Ministry and attended only by representatives of Hecho,

Krupp and Rochling. At this second meeting it was stated that the Nazi Party had informed the industrialists that the war was practically lost but that it would continue until a guarantee of the unity of Germany could be obtained. German industrialists must, through their exports, increase the strength of Germany. They must also prepare themselves to finance the Nazi Party which would be forced to go underground as Maquis (in Gebirgaverteidigungastellen gehen).

From now on the government would allocate large sums to industrialists so that each could establish a secure post-war foundation in foreign countries. Existing financial reserves in foreign countries must be placed at the disposal of the Party so that a strong German Empire could be created after the defeat.

It was also immediately required that the large factories in Germany create small technical offices or research bureaus which would be absolutely independent and have no known connection with the factory. These bureaus would receive the plans and drawings of new weapons as well as whatever documents they needed to continue their research, and which must not be allowed to fall into the hands of the enemy. These offices are to be established in large cities where they can be most successfully hidden as well as in little villages near sources of hydro-electric power where they can pretend to be studying the development of water resources. The existence of these is to be known only by very few people in each industry and by chiefs of the Nazi Party. Each office will have a liaison agent with the Party. As soon as the Party becomes strong enough to re-establish its control over Germany the industrialists will be paid for their effort and cooperation with concessions and orders.

4. These meetings seem to indicate that the prohibition against the export of capital which had been rigorously enforced had been completely withdrawn and replaced by a

new Nazi policy whereby industrialists with government assistance would export as much of their capital as possible. Previously exports of capital by German industrialists to neutral countries had to be accomplished rather surreptitiously and by means of special influence.

Now the Nazi party would stand behind the industrialists and urge them to save themselves by getting funds outside Germany, at the same time advancing the party's plans for its post-war operation. This freedom given to the industrialists further cemented their relations with the Party by giving them a measure of protection.

5. The German industrialists are not only buying agricultural property in Germany but are placing their funds abroad, particularly in neutral countries. Two main banks through which this export of capital operates are the Basler Handelsbank and the Schweizerische Kreditanstalt of Zurich. Also there are a number of agencies in Switzerland which for a 5 percent commission buy property in Switzerland, using a Swiss cloak.

6. After the defeat of Germany the Nazi Party recognises that certain of its best known leaders will be condemned as war criminals. However, in cooperation with the industrialists, it is arranging to place its less conspicuous but most important members in positions with various German factories as technical experts or members of its research and designing offices.

For the A.C. of S., G-2.
WALTER K. SCHWINN
G-2, Economic Section
Prepared by
MELVIN M. FAGEN

To quote from the Article from the Daily Mail published on 9th May 2009 By Adam Lebor
http://www.dailymail.co.uk/news/article-1179902/Revealed-The-secret-report-shows-Nazis-planned-Fourth-Reich--EU.html

Revealed - The secret report that shows how the Nazis planned a Fourth Reich ... the EU[7]

The paper is aged and fragile, the typewritten letters slowly fading. But US Military Intelligence report EW-Pa 128 is as chilling now as the day it was written in November 1944.

The document, also known as the Red House Report, is a detailed account of a secret meeting at the Maison Rouge Hotel in Strasbourg on August 10, 1944. There, Nazi officials ordered an elite group of German industrialists to plan for Germany's post-war recovery, to prepare for the Nazis' return to power and work for a 'strong German empire'. In other words: the Fourth Reich.

Plotters: SS chief Heinrich Himmler with Max Faust, engineer with Nazi-backed company I. G. Farben

The three-page, closely typed report, marked 'Secret', copied to British officials and sent by air pouch to Cordell Hull, the US Secretary of State, detailed how the industrialists were to work with the Nazi Party to rebuild Germany's economy by sending money through Switzerland.

They would set up a network of secret front companies abroad and wait until conditions were right before taking over Germany again.

The industrialists included representatives of Volkswagen, Krupp and Messerschmitt. Officials from the Navy and Ministry of Armaments were also at the meeting and, with incredible foresight, they decided together that the Fourth German Reich, unlike its predecessor, would be an economic rather than a military empire – but not just German.

Nazi Germany exported massive amounts of capital through neutral countries and German businesses set up a network of front companies abroad. The German economy soon recovered after 1945.

The Third Reich was defeated militarily, but powerful Nazi-era bankers, industrialists and civil servants, reborn as democrats, soon prospered in the new West Germany. There they worked for a new cause; European economic and political integration.

Is it possible that what the Fourth Reich Nazi industrialists foresaw has, in some part at least, come to pass?

The Red House Report was written by a French spy who was at the meeting in Strasbourg in 1944 – and it paints an extraordinary picture.

The industrialists gathered at the Maison Rouge Hotel waited expectantly as SS Obergruppenfuhrer Dr Scheid began the meeting. Scheid held one of the highest ranks in the SS, equivalent to Lieutenant General. He cut an imposing figure in his tailored grey-green uniform and high, peaked cap with silver braiding. Guards were posted outside and the room had been searched for microphones.

There was a sharp intake of breath as he began to speak. "German industry must realise that the war cannot be won," he declared. "It must take steps in preparation for a post-war commercial campaign." Such defeatist talk was treasonous - enough to earn a visit to the Gestapo's cellars, followed by a one-way trip to a concentration camp.

But Scheid had been given special license to speak the truth as the future of the Reich was at stake. He ordered the industrialists to 'make contacts and alliances with foreign firms, but this must be done individually and without attracting any suspicion'.

After the war Scheid disappeared.

Scheid told the industrialists they were to borrow substantial sums from foreign countries after the war. They were especially to exploit the finances of those German firms that had already been used as fronts for economic penetration abroad. He cited the American partners of the steel giant Krupp as well as Zeiss, Leica and the Hamburg-America Line shipping company.

But as most of the industrialists left the meeting, a handful were beckoned into another smaller gathering, presided over by Dr. Bosse of the Armaments Ministry. There were secrets to be shared only with the elite of the elite.

Bosse explained how, even though the Nazi Party had informed the industrialists that the war was lost, resistance against the Allies would continue until a guarantee of German unity could be obtained. He then laid out the secret three-stage strategy for the Fourth Reich.

In stage one, the industrialists were to prepare themselves to finance the Nazi Party, which would be forced to go underground as a Maquis, using the term of the French resistance.

Stage two would see the government allocating large sums to German industrialists to establish a secure post-war foundation in foreign countries, while 'existing financial reserves must be placed at the disposal of the party so that a strong German empire can be created after the defeat.

In stage three, German businesses would set up a 'sleeper' network of agents abroad through front companies, which were to be covers for military research and intelligence, until the Nazis returned to power.

"The existence of these is to be known only by very few people in each industry and by chiefs of the Nazi Party," Bosse announced.

"Each office will have a liaison agent with the party. As soon as the party becomes strong enough to re-establish its control over Germany, the industrialists will be paid for their effort and co-operation by concessions and orders.'

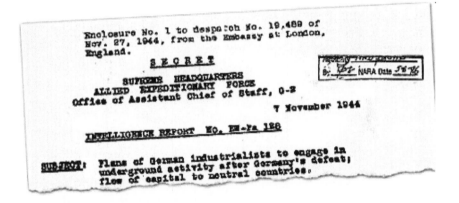

Extraordinary revelations: The 1944 Red House Report, detailing 'plans of German industrialists to engage in underground activity'.

The exported funds were to be channeled through two banks in Zurich, or via agencies in Switzerland which bought property in Switzerland for German concerns, for a five per cent commission.

The Nazis had been covertly sending funds through neutral countries for years.

Swiss banks, in particular the Swiss National Bank, accepted gold looted from the treasuries of Nazi-occupied countries. They accepted assets and property titles taken from Jewish businessmen in Germany and occupied countries, and supplied the foreign currency that the Nazis needed to buy vital war materials.

Swiss economic collaboration with the Nazis had been closely monitored by Allied intelligence.

The Red House Report's author notes: 'Previously, exports of capital by German industrialists to neutral countries had to be accomplished rather surreptitiously and by means of special influence'.

'Now the Nazi Party stands behind the industrialists and urges them to save themselves by getting funds outside Germany and at the same time advance the party's plans for its post-war operations.'

The order to export foreign capital was technically illegal in Nazi Germany, but by the summer of 1944 the law did not matter.

More than two months after D-Day, the Nazis were being squeezed by the Allies from the west and the Soviets from the east. Hitler had been badly wounded in an assassination attempt. The Nazi leadership was nervous, fractious and quarrelling.

During the war years the SS had built up a gigantic economic empire, based on plunder and murder, and they planned to keep it.

A meeting such as that at the Maison Rouge would need the protection of the SS, according to Dr. Adam Tooze of Cambridge University, author of 'Wages of Destruction: The Making And Breaking Of The Nazi Economy'.

He says: 'By 1944 any discussion of post-war planning was banned. It was extremely dangerous to do that in public. But the SS was thinking in the long-term. If you are trying to establish a workable coalition after the war, the only safe place to do it is under the auspices of the apparatus of terror.'

Shrewd SS leaders such as Otto Ohlendorf were already thinking ahead.

As commander of Einsatzgruppe D, which operated on the Eastern Front between 1941 and 1942, Ohlendorf was responsible for the murder of 90,000 men, women and children.

A highly educated and intelligent lawyer and economist, Ohlendorf showed great concern for the psychological welfare of his extermination squad's gunmen: he ordered that several of them should fire simultaneously at their victims, so as to avoid any feelings of personal responsibility.

By the winter of 1943 he was transferred to the Ministry of Economics. Ohlendorf's ostensible job was focusing on export trade, but his real priority was preserving the SS's massive pan-European economic empire after Germany's defeat.

Ohlendorf, who was later hanged at Nuremberg, took particular interest in the work of a German economist called Ludwig Erhard. Erhard had written a lengthy manuscript on the transition to a post-war economy after Germany's defeat. This was dangerous, especially as his name had been mentioned in connection with resistance groups.

But Ohlendorf, who was also chief of the SD, the Nazi domestic security service, protected Erhard as he agreed with his views on stabilising the post-war German economy. Ohlendorf himself was protected by Heinrich Himmler, the Chief of the SS.

Ohlendorf and Erhard feared a bout of hyper-inflation, such as the one that had destroyed the German economy in the Twenties. Such a catastrophe would render the SS's economic empire almost worthless.

The two men agreed that the post-war priority was rapid monetary stabilisation through a stable currency unit, but they realised this would have to be enforced by a friendly occupying power, as no post-war German state would have enough legitimacy to introduce a currency that would have any value.

That unit would become the Deutschmark, which was introduced in 1948. It was an astonishing success and it kick-started the German economy. With a stable currency, Germany was once again an attractive trading partner.

The German industrial conglomerates could rapidly rebuild their economic empires across Europe.

War had been extraordinarily profitable for the German economy. By 1948, despite six years of conflict, allied bombing and post-war reparations payments, the capital stock of assets such as equipment and buildings was larger than in 1936, thanks mainly to the armaments boom.

Erhard pondered how German industry could expand its reach across the shattered European continent. The answer was through supra-nationalism – the voluntary surrender of national sovereignty to an international body.

Germany and France were the drivers behind the European Coal and Steel Community (ECSC), the precursor to the European Union. The ECSC was the first supranational organisation, established in April 1951 by six European states. It created a common market for coal and steel which it regulated. This set a vital precedent for the steady erosion of national sovereignty, a process that continues today.

But before the common market could be set up, the Nazi industrialists had to be pardoned and Nazi bankers and officials reintegrated. In 1957, John J. McCloy, the American High Commissioner for Germany, issued an amnesty for industrialists convicted of war crimes.

The two most powerful Nazi industrialists, Alfried Krupp of Krupp Industries and Friedrich Flick, whose Flick Group eventually owned a 40 per cent stake in Daimler-Benz, were released from prison after serving barely three years.

Krupp and Flick had been central figures in the Nazi economy. Their companies used slave labourers like cattle, to be worked to death.

The Krupp company soon became one of Europe's leading industrial combines.

The Flick Group also quickly built up a new pan-European business empire. Friedrich Flick remained unrepentant about his wartime record and refused to pay a single Deutschmark in compensation. He died in July 1972 at the age of 90, leaving a fortune of more than $1billion, the equivalent of £400 million at the time.

'For many leading industrial figures close to the Nazi regime, Europe became a cover for pursuing German national interests after the defeat of Hitler,' says historian Dr. Michael Pinto-Duschinsky, an adviser to Jewish former slave labourers.

The continuity of the economy of Germany and the economies of post-war Europe is striking. Some of the leading figures in the Nazi economy became leading builders of the European Union.

Numerous household names had exploited slave and forced labourers including BMW, Siemens, and Volkswagen, which produced munitions and the V1 rocket.

Slave labour was an integral part of the Nazi war machine. Many concentration camps were attached to dedicated factories where company officials worked hand-in-hand with the SS officers overseeing the camps.

Like Krupp and Flick, Hermann Abs, post-war Germany's most powerful banker, had prospered in the Third Reich. Dapper, elegant and diplomatic, Abs joined the board of Deutsche Bank, Germany's biggest bank, in 1937. As the Nazi empire expanded, Deutsche Bank enthusiastically 'Aryanised' Austrian and Czechoslovak banks that were owned by Jews.

By 1942, Abs held 40 directorships, a quarter of which were in countries occupied by the Nazis. Many of these

Aryanised companies used slave labour and by 1943 Deutsche Bank's wealth had quadrupled.

Abs also sat on the supervisory board of I.G. Farben, as Deutsche Bank's representative. I.G. Farben was one of Nazi Germany's most powerful companies, formed out of a union of BASF, Bayer, Hoechst and subsidiaries in the Twenties.

It was so deeply entwined with the SS and the Nazis that it ran its own slave labour camp at Auschwitz, known as Auschwitz III, where tens of thousands of Jews and other prisoners died producing artificial rubber.

When they could work no longer, or were verbraucht ('used up' in the Nazis' chilling term), they were moved to Birkenau. There they were gassed using Zyklon B, the patent for which was owned by I.G. Farben.

But like all good businessmen, I.G. Farben's bosses hedged their bets.

During the war the company had financed Ludwig Erhard's research. After the war, 24 I.G. Farben executives were indicted for war crimes over Auschwitz III but only twelve of the 24 were found guilty and sentenced to prison terms ranging from one-and-a-half to eight years. I.G. Farben had got away with mass murder.

Abs was one of the most important figures in Germany's post-war reconstruction. It was largely thanks to him that, just as the Red House Report exhorted, a 'strong German empire' was indeed rebuilt, one which formed the basis of today's European Union.

Abs was put in charge of allocating Marshall Aid – reconstruction funds – to German industry. By 1948 he was effectively managing Germany's economic recovery.

Crucially, Abs was also a member of the European League for Economic Co-operation, an elite intellectual pressure group set up in 1946. The league was dedicated to the establishment of a common market, the precursor of the European Union.

Its members included industrialists and financiers and it developed policies on monetary integration and common transport, energy and welfare systems that are strikingly familiar today.

When Konrad Adenauer, the first Chancellor of West Germany, took power in 1949, Abs was his most important financial adviser.

Behind the scenes Abs was working hard for Deutsche Bank to be allowed to reconstitute itself after decentralisation. In 1957 he succeeded and he returned to his former employer.

That same year the six members of the ECSC signed the Treaty of Rome, which set up the European Economic Community. The Treaty further liberalised trade and established increasingly powerful supranational institutions including the European Parliament and European Commission.

Like Abs, Ludwig Erhard flourished in post-war Germany. Adenauer made Erhard Germany's first post-war economics minister. In 1963 Erhard succeeded Adenauer as Chancellor for three years.

But the German economic miracle – so vital to the idea of a new Europe – was built on mass murder. The number of slave and forced labourers who died while employed by German companies in the Nazi era was 2,700,000.

Some sporadic compensation payments were made but German industry agreed a conclusive, global settlement only in 2000, with a £3billion compensation fund. There was no admission of legal liability and the individual compensation was paltry.

A slave labourer would receive 15,000 Deutschmarks (about £5,000), a forced labourer 5,000 (about £1,600). Any claimant accepting the deal had to undertake not to launch any further legal action.

To put this sum of money into perspective, in 2001 Volkswagen alone made profits of £1.8billion.

But the Red House Report is a bridge from a sunny present to a dark past. Joseph Goebbels, Hitler's propaganda chief, once said: 'In 50 years' time nobody will think of nation states.'

For now, the nation state endures. But these three typewritten pages are a reminder that today's drive towards a European federal state is inexorably tangled up with the plans of the SS and German industrialists for a Fourth Reich – an economic rather than military imperium.

'The Budapest Protocol', Adam LeBor's thriller inspired by the Red House Report, is published by Reportage Press.
How valid is all this?

You can check for yourself. What I have done is put the evidence in a line and looked along it to see where it points.
(See also eu-facts.org appendix 35).

Starting off as European Coal and Steel In 1951, the Treaty of Paris was signed, creating the European Coal and Steel Community (ECSC).

The Treaty of Paris was an international treaty based on international law, designed to help reconstruct the economies of the European continent, prevent war in Europe and ensure a lasting peace.

The Treaty of Rome was signed in 1957, when Monnet was President of the French Parliament. It morphed into the European Economic Community in 1964 with Hallstein elected as President to implement the 1944 project. The 1942 German EWG document seems to have been used as a first draft of the post war European Economic Community after 1964 by the 5 German bureaucrats on that committee (all of whom had worked enthusiastically for Hitler) and had not been deNazified. Walter Hallstein was made president of the committee by Adenauer. Although never in the Nazi Party, Adenauer as Mayor of Cologne was an open supporter of the Nazis.

Frenchman Jean Monnet began to push the concept of the EU as soon as the war ended, leading to the Treaty of Rome in 1957 signed by Belgium, France, Italy, Luxembourg, the Netherlands and West Germany. It was the precursor to the EU.

Under the patronage of Adenauer, Walter Hallstein later became the first president of the European Commission in 1958 before it was renamed as the European Union. He was also made the State Secretary for Foreign Affairs for Germany in the immediate post war years.

≈4≈

1958 - 1964

In 1964 Germany appointed a committee under Holstein to exploit that hidden wealth to hijack the embryonic EU. No details are available of their deliberations but possibly they used wholesale bribery, offers that could not be refused, or just being paymaster to impose their 1944 plan. 'He who pays the piper calls the tune' with their hidden stolen wealth

They described the 1957 EEC as 'our Brussels EU' inferring that they felt they owned it. Whatever they did, they did it successfully. We now have the resulting undemocratic EU now based on the 1942 *Europaische Wirtschafts Gemeinsschaft* still using civic bribery. If an ex-EU bureaucrat with a lucrative EU pension does or says anything considered detrimental to the EU they can revoke his pension. *(Appendix 9)*

Although Monnet had been lobbying for years for an EU and successfully got the Treaty of Rome signed, the real 'father of the EU' was OberGruppenfuhrer Dr Scheid, Chairman of the 1944 committee, as it was his plan that was eventually used by the early EEC.

Monnet was later given the accolade of 'father' of the European Union to hide the true founder, Dr Scheid.

Monnet's counsel concerning how the EU should be achieved can best be summed up by simply paraphrasing what he said at the UN in 1952:

"The nations of Europe should be guided towards a supra-national state without their people understanding what is happening. This can be achieved by successive small steps, each disguised as having an economic purpose, which will eventually and irreversibly lead to a federation." This is known as the 'salami' technique.

Spaak proposed that the EU be always referred to as a 'Common Market' to disguise its true nature.

Spinelli advocated that the aim should be to stealthily assemble the components of a supranational government and only to declare its true purpose at the end of the process by unveiling a 'Constitution'. Thus the public would be deceived. The Lisbon Treaty is, in effect, the Constitution. By then it would be too late for the democratic peoples of Europe to do anything about it.

The EEC/EU 'Constitution' was very carefully crafted and worded to ensure that once a country became enmeshed there was no mechanism for them to withdraw without overcoming truly daunting hurdles. All national democratic structures were to be dismantled and full political control passed to the undemocratic and unelected EU in Brussels. National identities were to be abolished. England would no longer exist.

Hallstein and the EU committee clearly used the 1942 document as the first draft for what was to become the EU.

It would not be far from the truth to describe the EU as a reconstituted Fourth German Reich but with much Frankfurt School influence.

Who was who in Germany's "Brussels EU"?

From the beginning, one of the main financiers of the "Brussels EU" was the West German Government. On April 24, 1964, the key architects of the "Brussels EU" – all of them active members of the IG Farben/Nazi coalition during WWII – met at the "Brussels EU" headquarters to stake their claims on the future of the European continent. Apparently they were so sure that they would succeed in taking control of Europe in their 3rd attempt that they posed proudly for this picture. *(Appendix 5)*

The men shown in this picture are:

1. **EU Commission President Walter** Hallstein – the <u>boss </u>of the "Brussels EU".

2. **German Chancellor Ludwig Erhard.**

3. **Ludger Westrick**, Head of the German Chancellery.

4. **Karl Carstens**, German Secretary of State for the Ministry of Foreign Affairs.

5. **Karl-Günther von Hase**, Head of the Press and Information Service of the German government.

What were their backgrounds? To quote from EUfacts:

1. **Walter Hallstein,**a German lawyer, had been appointed the founding president of the so-called EU Commission, the highest body within the "Brussels EU." In 1964, when this meeting took place, he had already been the chief architect of the "Brussels EU" construct for seven years. Hallstein, not legitimized by any democratic vote anywhere in Europe, ruled like a "tsar" – imposed by the successors of the IG Farben oil and drug cartel – over an

army of 3,000 administrative servants in Brussels and a budget of billions of Euros (in today's currency).

2. Before and during WWII Hallstein had served the Nazi regime as a fervent advocate of Nazi law, including at the University of Rostock, Germany. In January 23, 1939, three years after his Nazi law colleagues had issued the Nuremberg racial laws – and only months before the Nazi/IG Farben coalition launched WWII by attacking Poland – Hallstein talked about future European law under German leadership ("Rechtseinheit Großdeutschlands"). He left no doubt to whom his loyalty belonged, saying that: "One of the most important laws (in Nazi occupied European countries) is the protection Law for German blood and honour."

3. **Ludwig Erhard** had been an economic consultant to the Nazi/IG Farben-coalition. He was the founder and head of the Nazi-financed "Institut für Industrieforschung" ("Institute for Industry Research") from 1942. Erhard was never a committed Nazi but as an exceptionally gifted economist he was useful to them. He had to tread very carefully and had he not gone along with the Nazis he would have probably ended up in a concentration camp. It must have been a very difficult time for him. Post war he was instrumental in Germany's recovery.

4. After World War II, Erhard became an economic consultant to the Allied forces and later to the Minister of Economic Affairs and Chancellor in post-war Germany. He was then a member of the Christian Democratic Party (CDU). In his functions, he was responsible for the reintegration of the IG Farben managers sentenced in Nuremberg for crimes against humanity into leading corporate positions in post-war Germany.

One of those to be "reintegrated" was BAYER's WWII director Fritz Ter Mer. This executive of the world's largest pharmaceutical (!) company was convicted at the

Nuremberg War Crimes Tribunal No. VI - for genocide in connection with the deadly human experiments with patented Bayer drugs in KZ Auschwitz (www.profit-over-life.org). With the help of Erhard – then Germany's Minister of Economic Affairs – Ter Mer was released from prison and reinstated as the chairman of the board of BAYER by 1956.

Erhard publicly defended such an unspeakable act by stating that the selection of Germany's post-war industry captains was necessary because of their "expertise in the field of economics and chemical technology". Obviously, it did not bother Erhard that Ter Mer and the other pharmaceutical drug lords had been tried in Nuremberg for war crimes. As part of the "give and take", Erhard was rewarded with the appointment as vice-chancellor of Germany only one year later.

5. **Ludger Westrick** was Chairman of the Board, President, and later Central Trustee of the state-owned "Vereinigte Industrie-Unternehmen AG" (VIAG) during the Nazi era. In post-war Germany, Westrick joined the Christian Democratic Party (CDU).

By 1964 – at the time of the above meeting – he had been appointed head of the German Chancellery, one of the most powerful positions in the German political system. In that function he controlled all the key decisions of German politics, including economics, foreign policy, secret service, political funds, public relations and propaganda of the post-WWII German government.

Westrick's predecessor as head of the German chancellery – and the man who had coordinated the political and financial support for Hallstein and the construction of the "Brussels EU" from the German chancellery for the first 6 years of the new European politburo of the cartel in Brussels – was Hans Globke. Globke was a key figure in Hitler's Ministry of Internal

Affairs. He was the lawyer who was responsible for implementing Nazi laws and regulations, subjugating the occupied countries of Europe under the rule of the IG Farben/Nazi coalition. Moreover, Globke was co-author of the legal codex that made the Nuremberg racial laws binding law in Nazi Germany. This codex formed the legal basis for the annihilation of Jewish, Slavic and other people in Nazi occupied Europe. The second author of this codex, Wilhelm Stuckart, was a State secretary in the German Interior Ministry and was one of the selected few participants of the infamous "Wannsee Conference" that decided the extermination of more than 10 million Jewish people.

Westrick, the man in the picture above, was the immediate successor of Globke and had been introduced into his office by this man.

6. **Karl Carstens** was an enthusiastic Nazi follower, joining the SA in 1934. He was a registered member of the Nazi party, the NSDAP, from 1940 on. In 1955 he became a member of the German Christian Democratic Union.

   In 1954 Carstens joined the German Foreign Service and from 1955 he was the official standing representative of the German Federal Republic at the European Council in Strasbourg! Concurrently, he advanced to the position of Vice-Minister of Foreign Affairs with the defined field of responsibility: "European Questions."

   In 1958 he advanced the Head of the Division "Europe West" within the German Ministry of Foreign Affairs.

7. **Karl-Günther von Hase** joined the Wehrmacht, the German army, in 1936. He participated in the Nazi-German Invasion of Poland in 1939, the Battle of

France in 1940 and the Invasion of Russia from 1941 to 1945, and married the daughter of a Nazi-General. After the war, von Hase joined a diplomatic school in the Federal Republic of Germany and started a blitz-career in German politics. From 1962 to 1967 – including the time of the above meeting in Brussels – von Hase was head of the press office of the German government and responsible for its public relations and propaganda.

How did these bureaucrats, who were so involved with Nazi projects, come to have such prominent and influential positions post war?

Follow the money. The vast sums of stolen money hidden outside of Germany in the dying days of WWII.

The Frankfurt School quietly developed their philosophy in the universities of the USA and the UK. Their big chance came during the Vietnam War and the turmoil it caused in the university campuses of the US and UK. Such academics as Saul Alinsky had a very big influence on Obama and Clinton. Many University academics now support this philosophy and it is difficult to get a University teaching post unless you support it too. *(Appendix 8)*

It became known as the Age of Aquarius and of Liberated Personal Freedom, whereas, in reality the covert Frankfurt School of Marxism was beginning to have an effect. *(Appendix 3)*

While it has no 'Mr Big' or Bible/Koran/Mein Kampf, it is a philosophy that many intellectuals and politicians find very attractive indeed. It gives them unelected authority and unaccountability, secure jobs, good salaries and pensions, and an exaggerated sense of their own importance. Good for their egos. They can then order the disenfranchised citizens about without sanction.

≈5≈

1965 - 2016

The UK political elite decided that after the devastation of the war our democratic political system was no longer 'fit for purpose'. The covert Frankfurt School Marxism doctrine was becoming very fashionable among many of our intellectuals and political elite.

The Foreign and Commonwealth Office felt that Britain had been so bankrupted by the war and the loss of our empire that our influence in the world was at serious risk. The F&CO and the arrogant British political elite (such as Ted Heath, Peter Thornycroft, Geoffrey Howe, Sir Crispin Tickell and Geoffrey Rippon) felt that the only solution to maintain that influence was to join the EU – but they also felt that it was vital that the people of Britain were not informed of their intentions.

Tickell gave strict instructions to our MPs not to talk about what was being planned. Ted Heath was so keen on UK joining the EU that at a secret meeting with the French Premier Pompidou (which he did without even telling his cabinet what he was up to) he agreed to hand over nearly all UK fishing and UK satellite technology to France in exchange for France not objecting to UK joining. Black Arrow which put the world's third satellite into orbit was cancelled as the then British ministers considered 'satellites have no potential'?

The EU had to be introduced in thin salami slices so that the public would not notice until it was too late. By far the worst was that this notion became fashionable among the Permanent Secretaries and Cabinet Office. It is they who are unelected but being permanent are able to manipulate and deceive the short term elected ministers – and this continues today.

It is worth noting that many in the post war Old Labour Party were very uneasy with the EU concept due to its fundamentally undemocratic nature.

Before the war there was quite a strong body of opinion in the upper echelons of the British establishment who rather admired Hitler and were very ready to accommodate him. They were very condescending of the 'common citizens'. When the war was won the same people then felt that the Frankfurt School was the 'horse to back'. Their next generation have an even more sneering attitude to the lumpen citizens.

In 1970 Heath began to secretly manoeuvre the UK into the EU. However the unbelievably simple-minded, naive and incompetent UK negotiators, ever ready to compromise and appease, managed to ensure that British interests were seriously disadvantaged at all levels. The French negotiators, however, managed to ensure that French interests were always paramount and they made complete monkeys of the UK negotiators. From agriculture to fishing to the financial contribution by the UK, the British taxpayer has been paying grossly over the odds and getting a raw deal ever since. (*Appendix 58*)

The money needed to fund our roads, care homes, schools, hospitals, army etc. has been meekly handed over to the EU to squander.

Our political elite, blinkered, bloody minded managers (and their bean counters) and militant politically minded Unions have also aided and abetted the steady de-industrialisation of the UK since the end of the war.

The influence of the UK in the EU is virtually nil. The UK is always outvoted by at least 11 to 1 in the European Parliament. Usually more so as the LibDem and most of the Tory MEPs slavishly acquiesce to the EU. The UK is essentially little more than a cash cow for the European Commission.

The UK political elite of all three parties have been slowly moving the UK to the EU remit of an elected parliament with steadily reducing authority (but still with the pay and perks) and our sovereignty being steadily moved to Brussels. Our democratic institutions have been neutered in favour of bureaucratic control. Brexit will hopefully stop that.

The Lisbon Treaty allows the EU to change or revoke any signed agreements retrospectively without consulting any elected parties. It is an Enabling Act.

How was the Lisbon Treaty voted through our parliament without MPs seeing it or reading it? *(Appendix 40)*

We are continually given carefully constructed statements to deceive us. For example, when Gordon Brown came back from signing the Lisbon Treaty in Brussels he trumpeted that he had negotiated several Red Lines to protect British interests. 'Good ol' Gordon' we thought. 'That's the way to do it'. What he actually said was absolutely true. However he omitted to add the rest of the sentence that turned his statement on its head – the Red Lines would only last 5 years at most. Was that a lie or not? What he said was the truth albeit only part of the truth though deceitful in the extreme.

Remember the Lisbon Treaty is an Enabling Act and those Red Lines can be unilaterally revoked by the EU at any time.

Brown should, however, be given full credit for refusing to allow UK to join the Euro. It was a wise decision as the Euro has been an unmitigated disaster for many countries in the EuroZone.

The Soviet, the EU, the Frankfurt School and Hitler's National Socialist systems of government are, in practice, very similar indeed and attract a similar sort of people. The state is controlled by unelected wealthy elite with a complicit, unaccountable and overpaid (state bribery?) bureaucracy implementing their edicts. They all have a police force accountable to the state, not the people *(Appendix 14)*.

The EU is essentially a reincarnation of the Nazi 1942 *Europaische Wirtschafts Gemeinsschaft* combined with the Frankfurt School of Marxism.

As such it was very easy for the ex-National Socialist bureaucrats of Hitler to work post war with the EU Frankfurt Marxist bureaucrats for their own advantage and to the detriment of the general public.

The philosophy of Marx was to release the workers from the subjugation and oppression of the political elite of Russia and Victorian England. It is ironic that all Marxist governments end up being run by middle class elites who eventually become even more brutal oppressors of their 'working class' to maintain their control.

So far our military have been able to keep their ethos. However, when Romano Prodi was President of the EU (1999 – 2004), he said "there will be an EU army and only an EU army". EuroCorps intends to take over and absorb the British Armed Forces.

To this end the morale, capability and facilities of our armed forces are being steadily eroded by our own political elite. It will soon be at a point where the only option left will be to hand over our emasculated armed forces to EuroCorps as they will be incapable of functioning as a military unit. It will be unable to perform as it has traditionally due the appalling (deliberate?) political mismanagement, the shortage of manpower and lack of proper equipment.

Curiously again the EU also wants England to be divided into 9 Regions, thus removing the historic English Shires, and steadily being de-industrialised, e.g. the EU gave Ford £80million to transfer the Ford Transit production from Southampton to Turkey *(Appendix 10)*

There are many other unnerving coincidences with the EWG. The EU also intends to transfer most of the City of London Financial Services to Paris and Frankfurt and absorb the UK Armed Forces.

Mass immigration into the UK is essential to remove the notion of 'the English'. Not just the English but the French, Dutch and all the other nations of Europe. Promoted by Peter Sutherland – Ex European Commissioner, Director General of the World Trade organisation, ex-Chairman of Goldman Sachs, Steering Committee Bilderberg Group.

Peter Sutherland; *"We still nurse a sense of our homogeneity and difference from others, and that's precisely what the European Union, in my view, should be doing its best to undermine."*

Whether this mass immigration into the UK is a good or bad thing is not the point. It was initiated by Tony Blair deliberately without informing the British people of what he intended let alone asking their approval.

Most important is that immigration policy into the UK is controlled by Brussels – not by the British public. It is known as the EU Coudenhove Kalergi Plan *(Appendix 4)*. It is quite sinister and almost a James Bond film plot.

"I don't like them! (*white guys*) I want them to be the lost species in a hundred years!"

Yasmin Alibhai Brown said this on the 4 June 2006 edition of 'Dateline London.'

No BBC executive, politician, journalist, judge or policeman ever accused her of *'racism.'* Nor was she ever prosecuted for wanting the white race disappeared.

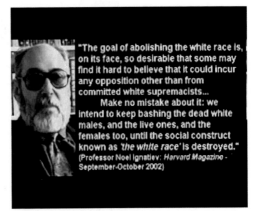

"The goal of abolishing the white race is, on its face, so desirable that some may find it hard to believe that it could incur any opposition other than from committed white supremacists...

Make no mistake about it: we intend to keep bashing the dead white males, and the live ones, and the females too, until the social construct known as *the white race* is destroyed."
(Professor Noel Ignatiev: *Harvard Magazine* - September-October 2002)

Jack Straw The English as a race are not worth saving *(Appendix 69)*

Van Rumpoy 'The EU intends to control all countries west of Russia If the public doesn't want EU expansion we do it anyway'.

Peter Mandelson said 'The democratic experiment in Europe has failed – time to move to the post democratic society'.

Trotsky invented the word 'racist' to browbeat dissenters, and Lenin's education guru Makarenko coined the term 'political correctness'. *(Appendix 63)*

G. Brock Chisholm
World Health Organization

"To achieve One World Government it is necessary to remove from the minds of men their individualism, their loyalty to family traditions and national identification."
Brock Chisholm, when director of the World Health Organisation. See *theeuroprobe.org* and type in; 2017-001 into the search box for 'White Tribes'.

Is the EU Democratic?

The BBC continually describes the EU as democratic. Well, is it?

What is the difference between a police state and a democratic state?

An Oligarchic/Police State

- An Oligarch of an unelected 'Elite' who are effectively the 'State'.
- Any elected parliament has no power.

- System run by a complicit Civil Service.
- No criticism of the State permitted.
- The State controls all social activities.
- Press and media controlled by the State.
- Police answerable to the State.
- Citizens monitored by State Security.
- Police can arrest anyone without needing a warrant or evidence.
- All citizens required to carry an ID card.
- Local informers report on neighbours.
- Citizens are guilty until they can prove their innocence.

A Democratic State

- Citizens can stand for any political position and vote for any party.
- The Civil Service is strictly neutral.
- Vote by secret ballot to remove or keep the government of the day.
- The government is required to give a truthful answer to any question.
- Citizens are innocent until proven guilty and arrested only with a warrant.
- Police and judiciary independent of government.
- Press and media free from government control.
- Citizens have freedom of speech, movement and religion.

Comparison of an Oligarchic/Police State with the EU

- Government by an unelected Elite who cannot be voted out - yes

- Any elected parliament has little or no power - yes
- System run by a pampered and compliant Civil Service - yes
- No criticism of State permitted - moving that way
- All commercial and social activities controlled by the State - desired
- Press and Media controlled by the State - moving that way
- Police and Security Forces answerable to the State - yes
- Citizens continually monitored by Security - coming
- Police can arrest anyone without a warrant or evidence - yes
- All citizens required to carry an ID card - yes
- Local informers to report on their neighbours - now in embryonic form (€30 Million allocated for this)
- Citizens are guilty until they can prove their innocence - yes – Corpus Juris
- Licences required for nearly every activity -   moving that way
- Officials are unaccountable and immune from prosecution - becoming more so

The Origins of the EU shows why *(Appendix 17)*.
As yet, much of the EU list is embryonic – but the clear conclusion is that this is a bloodless coup that has the potential to become a police state.

Vladimir Bukovksy, the 63-year old former Soviet dissident, who spent 12 years in Soviet prisons, fears that the European Union is on its way to becoming another Soviet Union. In a speech he delivered in Brussels, Mr Bukovsky called the EU a monster that must be destroyed, the sooner the better, before it develops into a fully-fledged totalitarian state *(Appendix 18)*.

Clearly, a structure is being set up that will be an authoritarian state. There will be no mechanism to prevent it, sooner or later, from becoming a full-blown police state.

The immediate appearance of such a police state is most unlikely. We could just drift into one via small increments (the well-established Euro-salami technique) with each step fully justified and reasonable at the time until the result has been achieved – by deliberate stealth or mere happenchance.

Excuses? We've many already – e.g. trade, political correctness, Health & Safety, anti-terrorist measures, economics and the all-encompassing 'security'.

Can the corrupt and anonymous elite of the EU/EU Commission be trusted not to take advantage of such a golden opportunity to systematically increase their undemocratic control over us? History does not suggest that we can – and the English Channel will not protect us this time.

Notably, the political elite running the Labour, Conservative and Lib-Dem parties all fully support the EU Agenda. They must, therefore, also wish to have a political structure that is rapidly approaching something very akin to an authoritarian or police state. Whether they realise it or not they are classic Trojan Horses.

The rank and file of their parties have yet to become even faintly aware of exactly of what is being quietly and remorselessly established in their name.

European Court of Human Rights

Europe has had a long history of abuse of Human Rights from the Feudal System, the Spanish Inquisition, the French Revolution and the Napoleonic code to Hitler's NSDAP and Stalin's Soviet Eastern European states.

The European Court of Human Rights was started after WWII from an initiative by Eleanor Roosevelt because of the appalling abuse of Human Rights in Europe during the Nazi era. This was before the appalling behaviour of Stalin became exposed as very similar to the behaviour of the Nazi party.

It initially consisted of 12 very respected and experienced judges. (*Appendix 28*)

Now the ECHR consists of 47 judges, many of whom are appointed more for their political opinions than their legal expertise. Many were also complicit in the legal system of East European countries in their communist past.
Initially the ECHR was a stand alone court before the EU was established. Since then it is being slowly hi-jacked by the EU. In theory the ECHR and the EU are quite separate institutions. The ECHR is strictly under the Council of Europe (CoE). However they both fly the same flag (actually not really a flag but a banner) and if a country is in the CoE then they required to 'voluntarily' sign up to the ECHR. In practice the ECHR is inextricably linked with the EU and the CoE and is steadily becoming an agent of the European Commission.
They wish to see it English Common Law replaced with the EU Napoleonic Corpus Juris. Many of the politically appointed 'judges' have little or no legal expertise of English Common Law and many are from the old communist East European states.

In Corpus Juris you can be arrested without evidence, held in custody for perhaps years without charge and you are deemed guilty until you can prove your innocence. If you are in prison that is almost impossible. There is no Habeas Corpus, right of silence or onus on the prosecution to prove your guilt.

The (unelected) European Commission intend that there should be a common legal system across the EU. That system will be Corpus Juris and English Common Law is to be replaced by CJ.

It is important to understand that the main remit of the European Court of Justice is to advance EU integration, not justice.

≈6≈

The EU Today

Further evidence regarding the EU as an anti-democratic state?

"There can be no democratic choice against the European treaties."

Jean-Claude Juncker
(European Commission President)

As the late Labour MP Tony Benn described the European Commission (EC): *"I can think of no body of men outside of the Kremlin who have so much power without a shred of accountability for what they do."*

'The democratic experiment in Europe has failed. Time to move on to the post democratic society,'

Peter Mandelson

Has Europe had enough of police states?

More than enough! It would seem, though, that the EU elite clearly think an authoritarian or potential police state to be a jolly good idea – it certainly will be for them.

Many of the political elite running the Labour, Conservative and Lib-Dem parties fully support the EU agenda. They must, therefore, also wish to have a political structure that's rapidly approaching something very akin to an authoritarian or police state. They are the Utilus Babulus of the EU. The Useful Idiots.

So were we lied to?

In 1972 Edward Heath said we were voting for the *European Common Market*, stating: "There are some in this country who fear that, going into Europe, we shall in some way sacrifice independence and sovereignty. These fears, I need hardly say, are completely unjustified."

He was lying and he knew perfectly well at the time he was lying. He was in possession of a letter from The Foreign and Commonwealth Office that stated clearly it was to transfer all UK sovereignty to Brussels *(Appendix 19)*

Of course, Ted Heath's lies, to quote the *Daily Mail* of December 2012, had: "Scarcely been mentioned at the previous General Election, and the British people had very little idea of what they were letting themselves in for, other than a trading arrangement that might make it easier for us to sell our goods to our Continental neighbours".

Heath later said the reason he had to lie was because he considered "The British people are too stupid to be involved in governing themselves," *(Appendix 19)*.

Nor, it seems, is this an uncommon view in today's EU. In February 2014 the *Daily Mail* quoted unelected European Commission vice-president Viviane Reding: *"Britons are too ignorant about Europe to vote in a referendum on the subject. The British debate about Europe is so distorted that people could not make an informed decision about whether or not to stay in the EU,"* she said.

So that's put us in our place and this document is to give the British citizens the relevant information.

How did we get to this state of affairs?

The origins of the EU go back much further than 1964 *(Appendix 17 for the full story)*.

The first draft plan for the EU was virtually copied from a 1942 document developed by German bureaucrats at a conference in Berlin chaired by Walter Funk. At that time they were confident Germany would win WWII

On the Fringes was a Walter Hallstein. He was not on that committee but he was a keen member of the National Socialist leaders' programme. He was later to become the first president of the Commission of the European Economic Community, and one of the founding fathers of the European Union.

A 1942 conference looked at how Germany would run Europe after the final victory, and the document that emerged called for a *Europäische Wirtschafts gemeinschaft* (European Economic Community)

Immigration

Part of the EU plan is to get rid of national identities. One way of doing that is by immigration and 'multiculturalism', a policy enthusiastically implemented by Tony Blair during his period in power.

To quote the *Daily Mail:* "Conman Blair's cynical conspiracy to deceive the British people and let in 2 million migrants against the rules: *(Appendix 39)*

Explosive new biography lays ex-PM's betrayal … Tom Bower's new book *Broken Vows: Tony Blair – The Tragedy of Power* lays bare how he presided over a silent conspiracy to change the face of the UK It reveals how Blair instructed ministers to wave tens of thousands of asylum seekers into the UK under cover of their being 'economic migrants'."

Could it be a deliberate EU policy?

Yes, it's called *The EU Coudenhove Plan*, which is linked with the UN project *The Wildlands* and *Agenda 21 now 2030* to control the world's population for the benefit of a small, obscenely wealthy group – the so-called 'New Illuminati'. *(Appendix 20)*

It also describes how to destroy white culture and eventually eradicate the 'White Caucasian Tribes of Europe' *(Appendix 4)*

The EU wants to change European nations' cultures by mass immigration.

As former French president Nicolas Sarkozy told his people: "The goal is to meet the challenge of racial interbreeding. Not to intermarry racially is bad for the survival of the country."

Each year the EU awards the Charlemagne prize to the politician who has done most to further closer integration and the Coudenhove plan. *(For a list of recipients see Appendix 4 and 42).*

That challenge is being faced right now by Germany *(Appendix 21).*

Lenin and Stalin wanted to change Russian culture to that of Soviet culture. That was achieved by sending in troops in to confiscate the stored food and next year's seed condemning millions of small farmers (the Kulaks who were the backbone of Russian culture) to starvation.

The EU wants to eliminate the various cultures of Europe to produce a common European culture. They intend to do that by mass immigration and systematically squeeze out existing national cultures a small bit at a time.

National identity?

The concept is incompatible with the EU Project.

For example, under the EU's *Toine Manders Plan*, there cannot be an England rugby, cricket or football team as England will eventually cease to exist if we stayed in the EU *(Appendix 22).*

The new EU map omitted "England" and showed just 9 Regions instead. Clegg at that time stated that "England is not a legal entity within the EU".

EU has given us peace in our time?

This is just utter nonsense!

Peace was protected when in 1949 NATO was born via the Washington Treaty, signed by the most undamaged country (from WWII) and world power, the USA, along with Canada and *ten* Western European states — Britain, France, the Benelux countries, Iceland, Italy, Norway, and Portugal.

The key feature of that pact is a mutual defence clause: If one country is attacked, the others will come to its defence. However, when Argentina invaded Falklands no help came from EU, indeed France covertly collaborated with Argentina.

The EEC/EU didn't happen for another 8 years. So fast forward those 8 years to 1957 and the *Treaty of Rome*, where just *six* members set up the EEC that aimed to create: **"A common market, a customs union, plus free movement of capital and labour".** To please France it also promised subsidies to farmers, particularly the French farmers; a burden that most other EU nations carry today.

No mention of any 'defence'!

Farewell to a free press and freedom of speech.

The unelected European Commission intends to control all press and media by issuing an 'EU Press Card' to selected and accredited journalists. The EU will decide who can, and cannot, be a journalist in Europe. If journalists criticise the EU in reports, they'll risk having their press card confiscated. *Appendix 23)*

The seeds for this were sown in March 2001 when the European Court of Justice (ECJ) ruled that the EU could lawfully suppress political criticism of its institutions – and of its leading figures – sweeping aside English Common Law and 50 years of European precedents on civil liberties. *(Appendix 23).*

The ruling stated that the commission could restrict dissent and punish individuals who "damaged the institution's image and reputation".

The Spanish Advocate General of the EU Court of Justice has claimed that "Criticism of the EU is akin to blasphemy and could be restricted without affecting Freedom of Speech"

The ECJ found that the European Commission was entitled to sack Bernard Connolly, a British economist dismissed in 1995 for writing a critique of European monetary integration entitled *The Rotten Heart of Europe.*

Also the persecution of Stern reporter Martin Tillack *(Appendix 62)*

The ruling stated that the commission could restrict dissent and punish individuals who "damaged the institution's image and reputation". Whether or not they are telling the truth.

The Lisbon Treaty – A Dead Parrot Squawking?

This treaty is the European Constitution in disguise.

The Constitution was rejected by France, the Netherlands and Ireland: it should be a dead parrot, but the EC is keeping it on life support. They've changed the label on the tin, but the contents remain the same. The EU said that although those countries voted NO in their Referenda they really meant YES and ignored the result.

EU Constitution author and former French president Giscard d'Estaing admitted as much in July 2007 when he said: "In terms of its content, the Lisbon Treaty proposals remain largely unchanged; they are simply presented in a different way ... the reason is that the new text could not look too much like a constitutional treaty."

We take it that this was to fool the public?

It's also a 'Self-Amending Treaty' or 'Enabling Act' based on the 1933 German Enabling Act. The unelected EC can change anything in it retrospectively without involving any elected parliament. Yet the Lisbon Treaty was voted through the UK parliament without our MPs even seeing it, let alone reading it *(Appendix 25)*.

And former French Prime Minister Raymond Barre agreed: "I have never understood why public opinion about European ideas should be taken into account."

The Bold Gendarme

The British police are to be quietly superseded by Europol. A new paramilitary force, the Euro Gendarmerie, (EUROGENDFOR)[8] is being established – cloned from the French CRS (riot police). The latter gained a most unpleasant reputation for the brutal manner in which they suppressed civil unrest (*Appendix 26*).

The EU Arrest Warrant means you can be arrested without evidence and held without charge. You can be extradited to any country in the EU and held for an unlimited time without charge.

Whatever has happened to our police? As an example, London's Metropolitan Police have had a dossier for over 10 years alleging *prima facie* malfeasance and breach of their Royal Charter by the BBC from a member of the European Parliament (MEP). It has been decided it's not in the public interest to investigate this allegation.

---

[8] The organisation called the EUROGENDFOR, EGF, or more properly the European Gendarmerie Force, should be better known in Britain than it is, for its function is worrying and could affect this country in the future. *(Appendix 26)*

Britain's influence in the EU?

Voting in the EU Parliament is more farcical than voting in the Eurovision Song Contest.

Britain has 73 MEPs out of 751. This means that, even if all UK MEPs vote as one, we have less than 10% influence. Considering many UK MEPs slavishly vote with the EU, in reality we have about 3%.

We will always be outvoted, especially as we have now lost many of our vetoes. The EU Parliament often has to vote through dozens of laws by a show of hands at high speed with no count taken of votes.

Trade

It is claimed that if the UK were to leave the EU some 3 million jobs could be lost. This myth is based entirely on a 1999 report by the National Institute for Economic and Social Research (NIESR) that 3.2 million jobs were "associated" with exports to goods and services to the EU.

Yet NIESER director at the time, Martin Weale, has himself dismissed interpreting the 3 million associated jobs as job loss propaganda and "pure Goebbels" He's right, it's utter nonsense. The EU sells far more to the UK than we sell to them. The BBC allows people like Clegg to continually repeat it despite knowing full well it is incorrect. *(Appendix 47)*

The proposed TTIP and CETA are agreements to give overwhelming legal power to Corporates to gain control of such as NHS, Care Homes and large companies. Self-employed and independent traders are an anathema to the EU and they will be steadily squeezed out. It is their independence and difficulty to control that the EU hates. *(Appendix 72)*

About 70% of UK trade is with the rest of the world, but figures can be twisted. For example, say a UK company has a large export order to Brazil and it is sent in a shipping container. If the ship carrying it happens to call at Rotterdam to pick up more containers for Brazil, then that is counted as a UK export to the EU by our government -

although these are goods not destined for EU customers, just calling at an EU port in transit.

Reform of the EU

The EU *cannot* be democratically reformed from within.

The structure has been carefully set up in such a way so as to make that practicably impossible. David Cameron's laughable attempts to 'reform' even tiny bits of the EU met with the following front page comments:

"A farce" — the *Sun*

"The great delusion" — *Daily Mail*

"Cameron's EU deal is a joke" — *Daily Express*

"EU are joking" — *Metro*

"Ministers to defy PM on Europe" — *Daily Telegraph*

It effectively split the Tory party.

German finance minister Wolfgang Schäuble suggests Berlin would always have the final say on the financial plans of all countries within the Eurozone.

The Barmy EU army

The EU plans to take over the entire British Armed Forces. The European Commission intends there to be: "An EU army and *only* an EU army," according to former Commission President, and former Prime Minister of Italy, Romano Prodi.

UK armed forces now have poor housing, inadequate equipment, understaffing, shortages of essentials, disgraceful care of discharged troops, and training cuts (*Appendix 29*).

Considering our troops were sent to Iraq with obsolete equipment and totally inadequate desert clothing, it begs the question; Is the steady degradation of the morale our armed forces a deliberate policy to soften it up for easy transfer to EuroCorps? It certainly looks like it.

To quote Prodi again: "When I was talking about a European army I was not joking. If you don't want to call it an army, then call it 'Mary-Ann' or something."

There is a dog fight going on between the French and Germans as to who will run EuroCorps.

Innocent until proven guilty

English Common Law, where you are innocent until the *law* can prove your guilt, is to be replaced with EU *Corpus Juris*, where you are guilty until *you* can prove your innocence. Not easy when you are in custody.

As said earlier, under the European Arrest Warrant you can be arrested without firm evidence and detained for an unlimited time. *(Appendix 30),*

Trade Unions

The EU is steadily degrading collective bargaining – and is also considering being the only source of funding for political parties. Much of the unions' political influence comes from funding the Labour Party, which will almost disappear if such funding is banned. TTIP will give corporates massive legal advantages over workers.

And the opinion of the indomitable Bob Crow. (*Was the General Secretary of the National Union of Rail, Maritime and Transport Workers (RMT)*

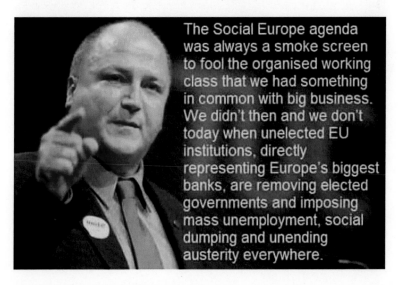

The Social Europe agenda was always a smoke screen to fool the organised working class that we had something in common with big business. We didn't then and we don't today when unelected EU institutions, directly representing Europe's biggest banks, are removing elected governments and imposing mass unemployment, social dumping and unending austerity everywhere.

The Pampered Executive or *Nomenklatura*

They are bureaucrats in plum jobs with excessive salaries, index-linked pensions and juicy perks who support the EU regardless. They are becoming more and more immune from accountability or dismissal for mismanagement, incompetence or corruption. Their task is to quietly enforce the EU agenda in the UK.

Surely blatant civic bribery?

The consequences of failing to continue to support the EU, even in retirement, can be dire. If a retired ex-EU official criticises the EU, it can revoke his pension. There are many with such pensioners in the UK's House of Lords...

What about the referendum?

It was a Labour manifesto promise but Blair refused to allow a referendum on EU membership.

That was despite his formal statement that the Labour manifesto was a "*Contract with the people.*" Labour's decision not to honour that promise was challenged in court and astonishingly the judge agreed with barrister Cecilia Lvimy, who argued: "They [Labour manifesto promises and contracts] are not subject to legitimate expectation," (*Appendix 31*).

Cameron was finally forced to run a referendum. His referendum has been held but there are powerful forces within the political elite who are actively working to thwart the democratic decision of the citizens.

The biased BBC and charities

The remit of the European Investment Bank is to fund organisations that "further the aims of the EU". They do not fund altruistically but only for the political gain of the EU.

The BBC receives many £ millions from the EU and has many Common Purpose alumni in positions of authority. (*Appendix 32*)

Many of our national charities and universities are also are in receipt of hundreds of thousands of Euros. If they do or say anything detrimental to the EU they can lose that funding; hence their very pro EU bias. It is essentially civic bribery e.g. the UK gives the EU £1 million of British taxpayers' money. The EU then gives a University a grant of £600,000 and keeps the rest. The University administrators think that is a good deal and the EU claims the credit. They can revoke that grant if the University does not advertise it is funded by the EU.

The Major problem with the BBC is that it only recruits via the extremist left wing Guardian newspaper. Unless an applicant espouses left wing views they will not be considered for any significant position. Especially so for any political position either up front on screen or radio or in the backroom programme production. Hence it's very left wing bias. *(Appendix 73)*.

Is it to be goodbye Blighty?

The cause of all European wars has been the leaders of sovereign powers competing for control of Europe. The European Union Project was proposed partly as a way to prevent further conflict and under it European countries will lose their sovereignty and be absorbed into a single undemocratic European State.

As for England, Wales, N. Ireland and Scotland, they will simply become 12 anonymous 'Regions of a Greater Europe' - each run by an unelected Regional Assemblies (RA). *(Appendix 77)*.

You will no longer be English, Irish, Welsh or Scottish, you will be European (*Appendix 17*).

Your Brave New Europe will be governed by "an unelected higher authority free from any control by elected politicians".

The unelected European Commission is that higher authority with members having virtually complete political control. Even today it's almost impossible to get rid of them, regardless of how corrupt, incompetent, or downright crooked they may be. The 'Committee of the Regions' in

Brussels will control the Regional Assemblies so our local councils would be completely neutralised. If we remained in the EU, our parliament would undoubtedly have survived in Westminster, but only as a token sideshow with no power.

Ken Clark has said he 'looks forward to the time when the Westminster Parliament is just a council chamber in Europe'.

How democratic is the European Parliament?

The elected European Parliament is little more than a rubber stamp agency for the European Commission and its Directives. Voting is by show of hands with rarely any counts taken.

Members of the European Parliament are pre-selected from a 'party list'. You then vote for the party, not the person. An independent, free-thinker, or maverick will find it almost impossible to get selected. The prime requisite will be their willingness to do what they are told.

Only large parties will be able to afford to stand for election. Smaller political groups are to be systematically squeezed out, leaving, perhaps, only three token, EU-compliant parties.

It is important to understand that the EU never acts directly in a country. It always acts by proxy through existing national institutions that have been hollowed out and filled with EU compliant staff.

The cost of the EU

This is so devious and convoluted that it is impossible to find out the true cost to Britain.

Every Briton contributes at least £1,000 a year in cash directly to Brussels – probably very much more. This does not include paying £5 for a piece of fish with your chips instead of £2.50, the extra costs of having to travel further to your Post Office, or the fines for petty infringements that flow from the 100,000-plus new EU laws – e.g.: fines for putting your dustbin out on the wrong day are not a direct EU rule but the consequence of EU rules pressurising the council. EU control exercised by proxy.

The crippling cost to our industry and commerce of inappropriate and unnecessary EU Directives can only be guessed at - then doubled or even trebled.

There are billions of Euros unaccounted for.

According to the 2014 report from the European Court of Auditors almost €7 billion of the EU budget was illegally spent in 2013. The ECA has declined to sign off EU spending for over 20 years, and its reports are a constant source of embarrassment to EU institutions. If this was any normal company the directors would be in jail. *(Appendix 33)*,

In total, EU spending in 2013 reached €148.5 billion, with regional policy and funds for rural development recording the highest error rates - 6.9% and 6.7% respectively of monies going astray.

So where are those € billions? Neil Kinnock was sent to Brussels to root out the corruption but one of the first things he did was to sack the EU Chief Account who exposed the corruption.

Where are we getting all this money from to fund the EU? Our Chancellors borrow £ billions each year which our children and grandchildren will have to pay back or transfer it from desperately needed projects in UK. The money to repair our roads, improve the NHS, care homes, housing and schools is sent to the EU.

ID cards

The only thing certain with ID cards is that they will not be the slightest hindrance to terrorists. ID cards are there to keep tabs on ordinary citizens.

Credit cards and store cards are ID cards and no problem. The ID cards that are suspect are those that store all-encompassing data about you that unaccountable bureaucrats have access to, and possibly many other individuals without you knowing. They can sell your health Data to, say, Insurance Companies. The government and police should not have any direct access to your ID card without approval by an authority completely independent of the Establishment.

Fishing and farming?

Edward Heath made a secret deal with the French to sacrifice the UK fishing fleet and satellite technology to the advantage of France. This was in exchange for France not blocking Heath's plot to trick the UK into joining the EU *(Appendix 34).*

The UK now has only some 11% of the EU fishing quota for the North Sea, and EU law makes British fishermen dump fish worth £ millions caught over their EU quota.

As Heath said at the time: "The British fishing industry has only 20,000 votes and is therefore not significant."

British fishing boats had to be burnt, thousands of fishermen lost their jobs and the price of imported fish doubled.

British fishing is now controlled by an unelected, unaccountable Maltese hotelier.

The Common Agricultural Policy

Set up to benefit French farmers prior to the EU accepting the UK's membership application. It's to the detriment of UK and other European countries farmers.

Asset stripping of Britain

A short list of financial and industrial FUBARs from the EU from can be found at; http://www.ukipdaily.com/good-eu-jobs-businesses/ with a few extras:

In the 1942 German document was the intent to asset strip UK and transfer all engineering and scientific activities to Germany. The following are just some of the modern day rape & pillage of UK industry aided and abetted by the EU:

- Heath handed France UK fishing and satellite technology to allow UK into EU.

- Cadbury moved factory to Poland 2011 with EU grant.

- Ford Transit moved to Turkey 2013 with EU grant.

- Jaguar Land Rover has recently agreed to build a new plant in Slovakia with EU grant, owned by Tata, the same company who have trashed our steel works and emptied the workers' pension funds.

- Peugeot closed its Ryton (was Rootes Group) plant and moved production to Slovakia with EU grant.

- British Army's new Ajax fighting vehicles to be built in SPAIN using SWEDISH steel at the request of the EU to support jobs in Spain with EU grant, rather than Wales.

- Dyson gone to Malaysia, with an EU loan.

- Crown Closures, Bournemouth (was METAL BOX), gone to Poland with EU grant, once employed 1,200.

- M&S manufacturing gone to far east with EU loan.

- Hornby models gone. In fact all toys and models now gone from UK along with the patents all with EU grants.

- Gillette gone to eastern Europe with EU grant.

- Texas Instruments Greenock gone to Germany with EU grant.

- Indesit at Bodelwyddan Wales gone with EU grant.

- Sekisui Alveo said production at its Merthyr Tydfil Industrial Park foam plant will relocate production to Roermond in the Netherlands, with EU funding.

- Hoover Merthyr factory moved out of UK to Czech Republic and the Far East by Italian company Candy with EU backing.

- ICI integration into Holland's Akzo Nobel with EU bank loan and within days of the merger, several factories in the UK were closed, eliminating 3,500 jobs.

- Boots sold to Italians Stefano Pessina who have based their HQ in Switzerland to avoid tax to the tune of £80 million a year, using an EU loan for the purchase.

- JDS Uniphase run by two Dutch men, bought up companies in the UK with £20 million in EU 'regeneration' grants, created a pollution nightmare and just closed it all down leaving 1,200 out of work and an environmental clean-up paid for by the UK tax-payer. They also raided the pension fund and drained it dry.

- UK airports are owned by a Spanish company.

- Scottish Power is owned by a Spanish company.

- Most London buses are run by Spanish and German companies.

- The Hinkley Point C nuclear power station to be built by French company EDF, part owned by the French government, using cheap Chinese steel that has catastrophically failed in other nuclear installations. Now EDF say the costs will be double or more and it will be very late even if it does come online. It could be done using the Rolls Royce Trident engines.

- Swindon was once our producer of rail locomotives and rolling stock. Not any more, it's Bombardier in Derby and due to their losses in the aviation market, that could see the end of the British railways manufacturing altogether even though Bombardier had EU grants to keep Derby going which they diverted to their loss-making aviation side in Canada.

- 39% of British invention patents have been passed to foreign companies, many of them in the EU.

- The Mini cars that Cameron stood in front of as an example of British engineering are built by BMW mostly in Holland and Austria. His campaign bus was made in Germany even though we have Plaxton, Optare, Bluebird, Dennis etc., in the UK. The bicycle for the Greens was made in the Far East, not by Raleigh UK, but then they are probably going to move to the Netherlands too as they have suggested recently.

- Fans outrage as foreign firm shrinks Terry's Chocolate Orange by 10 percent but price remains the same

Anyone who thinks the EU is good for British industry or any other business simply hasn't paid attention to what has been systematically asset-stripped from the UK. Name me one major technology company still running in the UK! I used to contract out to many, then the work just dried up as they were sold off to companies from France, Germany, Holland, Belgium, etc., and now we don't even teach electronic technology for technicians, due to EU regulations.

I haven't detailed our non-existent fishing industry the EU paid to destroy, or the farmers being paid NOT to produce food they could sell for more than they get paid to do nothing, don't even go there.

I haven't mentioned what it costs us to be asset-stripped like this, nor have I mentioned immigration or the risk to our security if control of our armed forces is passed to Brussels or Germany.

Also, Brussels offers British firms cash 'bribes' of almost £1,000 a time to take on foreign workers instead of British workers:

More can be found at: *(Appendix 74)*

≈7≈

The Future of the EU?

BRAVE NEW EUROPE AFTER 2016

"The nations of Europe should be guided towards a supranational state without their people realising what is happening. This can be achieved by small steps, each disguised as having an economic purpose, but which will eventually and irreversibly lead to a federation"

Jean Monnet,
(Acknowledged as the 'father' of the EU)

Europe is to be run by 'a higher authority free from control by elected politicians', i.e. the unelected European Commission. Any elected politicians will be completely neutralised. The EU will rule by coercion not by consent – similar to Stalin's and Hitler's governments.

We now have the political elite of the Frankfurt School and the political toffs of the US, EU and UK intending to come together to try to covertly establish a New World Order. This is to be run by the unelected, unaccountable, obscenely wealthy and privileged political elite, with elected parliaments neutered and the 'little citizens' returned to serfdom *(Appendix 15)*

Emblazoned on the wall in the EU Parliament's Visitors Centre are these words:

"National sovereignty is the root cause of the most crying evils of our times... The only final remedy for this supreme and catastrophic evil of our time is a federal union of the peoples..."

Why are the UK political elite so keen on the UK becoming absorbed into the EU? Where is their patriotism and loyalty to Britain, British history and the British public who elected them?

Always follow the money!

The elite and bureaucrats in the EU are grossly overpaid, with gold plated pensions and perks. There is virtually no restraint on petty (sometimes not so petty) corruption by them. Indeed they are encouraged to indulge in corruption. Once they get involved in minor corruption, such as fiddling expenses, they cannot get free of that tarnish and have to stay 'on message'. As previously mentioned, Neil Kinnock was sent to the EU to root out corruption but sacked the EU chief accountant for exposing the appalling leakage of money into many, many unaccountable projects. He is now a multi-millionaire.

Potential bureaucrats, who are deemed to be 'on message', are instructed and trained at public expense by Common Purpose[9] and to absorb the Frankfurt School philosophy. It is run by a Quasi Marxist administration. While not a secret organisation it is certainly very secretive. If a student is considered to have completed the course satisfactorily a suitable secure job is found for them. This is usually in a controlling administrative position in organisations such as the Police, local authorities, Fire Brigade, particularly the BBC, especially the Education

---

[9] *Common Purpose is a Charity based in Great Britain, which creates 'Future Leaders' of society. CP selects individuals and "trains" them to learn how society works, who pulls the "levers of power" and how CP "graduates" can use this knowledge to lead "Outside of Authority and the democratic process" (Appendix 16).*

Authorities and national Institutions. They are placed to quietly implement the Frankfurt School ethos.

The EU is also setting up Kaderschulen (schools for training of selected children, a kind of exclusive public schools paid for by the taxpayer) to train their offspring to be the next generation of unelected bureaucrats.

It is important to understand the EU never operates directly in a country. It operates by proxy through existing national institutions that have been hollowed out and stuffed with EU complicit bureaucrats who are bribed with excessive salaries and pensions 'so long as they stay on message'.

There are reported to be some 17,000 Common Purpose alumni in our institutions including some 600 in positions of control in the BBC *(Appendix 70)*.

Big businesses, which employ a lot of unskilled and semi-skilled workers, support the EU Directive of unrestrained immigration as it reduces their wages bill. It is also to degrade and eventually destroy the notion of English culture and nationhood. This 'low wage' economy is aided considerably by the dumbing down of our kids' education. They then have a pool of unemployed semi-educated Brits and immigrants to keep the wages down and earn big profits. It also enables them to pressurise the majority of middle class workers to work excessive overtime – often with no extra pay.

Big unions also support the idea of pan-EU unions as that will give the union leaders gold plated jobs for life as long as they 'stay on message' and give their full support to the EU rather than to their union members.

The EU intends to stop Collective Bargaining. They also want to be the sole funders of European political parties. The Unions get their influence by funding Labour. The EU will stop that.

Senior and influential but usually incompetent UK politicians, often past their 'sell by date', are frequently rewarded by being given an appointment to the unelected EU.

When their 'tour of duty' in the EU is over they then receive a very lucrative pension. If they subsequently do or say anything against the interests of the EU, their pension can be revoked. This is nothing less than state blackmail to muzzle them. Lord Chris Patten has an EU pension of some €30,000 a year so if he allows any criticism of the EU on the BBC he can lose that pension. Was he, therefore, a fit and proper person to run the so called 'unbiased' BBC? *(Appendix 38)*

Our House of Lords is stuffed with such people who know which way to vote to keep their juicy EU pensions but certainly not in the interests of the people of Britain.

We also have strange cases of MPs being very Eurosceptic when in opposition but becoming active supporters of the EU when in ministerial office.

This is usually down to 'an offer they cannot refuse'

Bribery? Blackmail? Suppression of press coverage or exposure of their corruption and personal habits? Or other strategies, such as slowly encouraging them to take more and more advantage of the slack security on expenses?

Once you have taken the Devil's Euro you are part of the system.

The United Nations Wildlands Project

The UN have unveiled their masterplan for the next 14 years – saying that they wish to implement global socialism and corporate fascism as part of their "Agenda 2030" plans. It should be remembered that the original UN Charter was written by Alger Hiss later exposed as a covert Marxist. Part of their plans, officially dubbed "Post-2015 Sustainable Development Goals," aims to reduce inequality worldwide by forcing individual governments and citizens alike to share their wealth under the guidance of a one world government. *(Apendices 52, 55 & 56)*

≈8≈

Post Brexit

Can we get Britain back *and our democracy with it?*

YES—all we need to do is repeal the 1972 European Communities Act. That can be done within 24 hours. Do not be deceived by arguments about Clause 50 of the Lisbon Treaty: it's a trap. It would take perhaps five years of negotiating giving the EU ample opportunity to prevaricate and keep kicking the can down the road, would need other EU members to agree, and carries horrendous financial penalties.

This is the path now chosen by Prime Minister, Theresa May and will begin by transferring all existing EU laws which currently apply in the UK en-bloc and then refine them in our own time through the democratic process.

Is there any other way? – Yes, Flexit. Not as good as repealing the 1972 Act but probably more achievable.

(More details of the options available are summarised at Appendix 60)

Clauses 50 describes how, if we wish, we can leave the EU but it would probably take over 5 years and enable the EU to spend millions of euros on spin, bribery and deception to ensure the UK public will be conned to stay in yet again.

No funding (as yet) will be available for an Exit Campaign and all the other member countries would have to agree to the country leaving. The financial penalties would also be horrendous.

It is also very important to understand what will happen if the UK wishes to leave the EU by implementing Clause 50. It will be decided upon by a committee of all the member countries except the UK, which will be excluded from those discussions and have no input into the decisions. Even if we were, we would be outvoted 26 to one *(Appendix 51 [ref 37])*. UK negotiators would be in a position of servility.

Brexit winning the Referendum has put a massive spanner in their works.

Clause 50 was not put in help countries to leave, but to make it incredibly hard with daunting penalties.

The UK still has the opportunity to withdraw by repealing the 1972 European Communities Act. However there is a very significant Quisling element in the House of Commons and House of Lords to overcome. There would be no financial penalties but it would take a major effort to disentangle the mess we are now in. Post Brexit negotiations with the rump of the EU could then be conducted from a position of strength not subservience. The Parliament Act may be needed to prevent the Lords, many with huge EU pensions, from blocking Brexit. UK negotiators here would be in a position of strength. *(Appendix 36)*.

The UK can then freely negotiate a Common Market Agreement with the EU, the Commonwealth and the rest of the world.

And finally…

For Every British Person To Read –This Is Your Life We're Talking About.

I respectfully request that the media stop their continued campaign to scaremonger about the Leave vote, and read the following letter to see the bullet we dodged.

From:
Sent: *Thursday, July 7, 2016 4:40 PM*
To:
Subject: *A Lucky Escape*

I know this is rather lengthy, but I hope that you will be able to publish all of this important set of facts for the public to see, given the amount of space allocated to Ken Harrison's letter.

Dear Viewpoint,

Having read the letters from those who did not agree with the result of the democratic vote for BREXIT, and myself having actually read the original Convention for an EU Constitution, and the two incarnations (2006 & 2007) of the Lisbon Treaty, I just have these points to make, given the obvious intent behind those treaties:

- *Never again would you be given the privilege of having a democratic vote, you would have had to accept every oppressive measure applied to you, without having a say in the matter. You would have given away any power you had under your control, because the EU*

Commission built an enabling clause into the treaty to allow it complete control.

- *You have had a lucky escape from what would have been the EU super state, sweeping away member states' country identities, with its Erasmus Exchange indoctrinating our young military and police to "Live Europe", possibly using neuro-linguistic programming, a brain washing technique.*
- ***This was kept secret from voters prior to BREXIT.*** *Germany and France created a 10 page plan, which 20 Ministers of the EU have already signed at secret meetings in Berlin and Paris.*
- *German Foreign Minister Frank-Walter Steinmeier said "A European superstate instead of the European Union", such an ultimatum will be presented to the countries which have not yet signed at the Visegrad Group (Czech Republic, Hungary, Poland, Slovakia) in Prague, to accept or get out of the EU.*
- *Those countries who's Ministers sign up to the superstate will be giving away their right to run their own countries i.e. their Sovereignty, and probably their government.*
- ***NO INDIVIDUAL MEMBER CRIMINAL LAWS****–Member states would have no right to a separate Criminal Code, only **EU Napoleonic Corpus Juris** (guilty until you prove yourself innocent) instead of our own **Constitutional Common Law** system with Habeus Corpus (innocent until proven guilty by a jury of your peers).*
- ***ARMED FORCES*** *– Germany and France propose the establishment of the body called **"European Security Compact"**, dealing with "all aspects of security and defence at the European level" "The EU should be able to plan and carry out both civilian and military operations in a more efficient manner, with the support of permanent **civil-military chains of command***

(EUROGENDFOR). The Union should be able to rely on constantly paid rapid reaction force and be able to provide joint funding mechanisms for such activities. Member states would have no right to their own army, their own special services."

- **NATO – The document also limits the role of NATO in the European continent.**

- **The EURO- When, not "if"** *– Member states would have no right to a separate tax system – including setting their own taxes. The development of the European Monetary Union will require – according to the authors – the intensification of the political process **as well as the division between the state(s), for the cost of the tax burden:** The common fiscal policy part of the new European Monetary Union "the missing cornerstone of the European Monetary Union" in practice must be understood as **a call to create a uniform tax system across all future European Union members, and reducing the existence of tax competition between countries.** Member states cannot have their own currency, or a central bank capable of defending the financial interests of the nation-state. (The Eurozone failed under these conditions, creating mass unemployment and poverty, and the EU State would take more and more from the richer members to prop up the monetary failures, raiding individual savings accounts has even been proposed.)*

- **NO SOVEREIGN CONTROL OVER THEIR OWN BORDERS – members would lose their right to run their own migration policy.** *To implement this policy, it is proposed to establish a "**first multinational border- and coast-guard**" to which Frontex by nation-states would delegate staff. Member States would actually lose control of their borders, and procedures for admission **and relocation of refugees on their territory.** The project also envisages the introduction of a uniform visa* *system and conduct of common foreign policy terms with other countries and international organizations.*

▪ **COMPULSORY DIVISION OF REFUGEES** – *The document also envisages sanctioning of **forced migration quotas for Member States**: "The situation in which the burden of migration is unevenly borne by a limited number of countries is not sustainable. First, the Dublin system has to be improved by providing permanent mechanisms linking and distribution of the burden of migrants between Member States."*

For those who doubt the veracity of this, which has been confirmed by London Daily Mail and The Express, you can find the original document in German at this URL https://www.superstation95.com/index.php/world/1534

*The UK must immediately leave the EU, trade freely under international rules and then negotiate with the EU - **but not on its own**. It must include all non EU countries and the British Commonwealth.*

Already the US Congress wants a swift trade deal with the UK and 11 other countries are lining up to conclude deals.

Parliament has a duty to follow through on BREXIT, and quickly, by implementing the Vienna Convention on the Law of Treaties 1969. This says the European Communities Act 1972 is void and of no legal force, before any of these measures are slipped in by Europhile Mandarins in Whitehall in positions of authority. Article 50 is a trap and a red herring to keep us in the burgeoning superstate.

Yours faithfully

Mrs J B
English Constitution Group

What of the future?

There are two conflicting World Orders which are impossible to accommodate with each other. The uncontrolled birth rate of the Third World is putting impossible strains on the First World with their inability to feed themselves. They want to freely share in the wealth that has been generated by 'Western Civilisation' as of right.

The current belief of the UN and the modern environmental movement is "anti-science, anti-technology, and anti-human." The radical environmentalists of today latch onto mythical assertions that have no basis in fact. However they support the idea that man is bad, man is the enemy of man, man is "destroying" the planet and the natural "balance" of nature. Sadly they have wedeled their way into positions of authority within the UN.

They want to be in absolute control of their version of a perfect, ordered society. *(Appendix 78)*

We currently have a society where traditional family life and one's ethnic and national history are of great importance to the individual. The desire to work to improve your life and family, individualism, personal freedom and free speech are highly prized. The individual has the opportunity to exploit their natural talents for the benefit of themselves and their family with spin-off for society in general.

Democratic governance is of prime importance for the individual as opposed to be the exclusive right of the political class. It can be somewhat chaotic but that is your choice.

The other is the United Nation's New World Order that want to supplant our culture with a rigid, controlled society.

With this philosophy all National borders, traditional family life, your ethnic heritage, private property and history are to be destroyed for a new society. This will be run by the 'New Illuminati'. A controlling Soviet style group of fabulously wealthy unelected politicians and bureaucrats. The Bureaucrats will be unelected and unaccountable to the citizens and appointed so long as they acquiesce to the New Illuminati. They will have a very pleasant life style if they stay 'on message'. The citizens will have no say whatsoever in governing.

Individualism and free speech are quite incompatible with such Soviet governance. The bulk of the population will be little more than serfs who will be controlled and ordered.

Individuals will be told what they can do, when they can do it, where can do it and how they can do it.

However everyone would be fed and housed but with no personal choice. All will be allocated by faceless bureaucrats.

The EU is part of this project.

The UN charter was written by Alger Hiss later exposed as a closet Marxist. The UN is now like a stick of Brighton rock. Sweet and sugary on the outside with Marxism running through its core.

This is been quietly set up over the last 50 years without consulting 'the people' or even informing them of the UN's intentions.

We can only have one of the above cultures.

It is like the fable of the fox meeting a farm dog. 'What are you doing?' said the dog 'Looking for some food' said the fox. 'Well join me here' said the dog. 'The farmer gives me food and a nice kennel to sleep in'. 'Sounds great' said the fox 'but what is that chain round your neck?" Well' said the dog 'the farmer only allows me to do what he wants when he wants it'. 'And the rest of the time?' asked the fox. 'Nothing I just sit in front of my kennel.' 'Not for me' said the fox 'I like to run free and do what I want – goodbye.

But of course the fox is a big threat to the smooth, orderly way of running the farm and has to be hunted down and killed.

APPENDIX

For the full documents control click on hyperlink

These books are must-reads if you want to know the full extent to which the citizens of the UK have been betrayed by our political elite *(Appendix 7)*.

- **'And into the Fire'** by Rodney Atkinson gives a far more detailed account of the EU.
- Ref 7 Speech by Rodney Atkinson to House of Commons
- **'The Great Deception'** by Booker and North. A very academic and detailed
- **'The Rotten Heart of Europe'** by Bernard Connolly.
- **The Nazi Roots of the 'Brussels EU'** The Rath Foundation

1 **Cost of EU** Almost €7 billion of the EU budget was illegally spent in 2013, the European Court of Auditors (ECA) revealed on Wednesday (5 November), as it declined to sign off EU spending for the 20th consecutive year.

https://euobserver.com/news/126405

2. Common Purpose

Common Purpose is a charity based in UK. It creates 'Future Leaders' of society and trains and teaches them how society works, who pulls the levers of power. How CP alumni can use that knowledge to lead outside of authority and pervert the democratic process.

It is a Marxist led organisation that trains bureaucrats funded by local authorities on how to covertly infiltrate the Frankfurt ethos *(Appendix 16, 44 & 67)* into UK institutions. It maintains its influence by ensuring that its alumni are given positions of unaccountable authority with gold plated salaries, pensions and perks so long as they stay 'on message'. If ever they make a complete and even dangerous mess of their job they will not be sacked – only moved sideways to a similar job or even promoted.

Appendix 16 *http://www.cpexposed.com/about-common-purpose*

Appendix 67
http://www.stopcp.com/bbcemployeescommonpurpose.php

Appendix 44 *http://www.cpexposed.com*

Leveson Inquiry has momentous implications for free speech. But Mail dossier raises disturbing questions about the influence of 'people who know best'

The driving force of Hacked Off is Sir David Bell – a founder of Common Purpose. The Objective of Hacked Off is to get all media under state control.
http://www.dailymail.co.uk/news/article-2233681/Leveson-Inquiry-Mail-dossier-raises-disturbing-questions-influence-quasi-masonic-nexus-people-know-best.html
　http://www.theeuroprobe.org/2015-074-common-purpose/
Video of Common Purpose by Brien Gerrish who has made a detailed study of CP.
https://www.youtube.com/watch?v=qd9qvbD3aOc&feature=youtu.be

3.　Frankfurt School
The ACW Review examined the corrosive work of the 'Frankfurt School' – a group of German-American scholars who developed highly provocative and original perspectives on contemporary society and culture, drawing on Hegel, Marx, Nietzsche, Freud, and Weber. Not that their idea of a 'cultural revolution' was particularly new. 'Until now', wrote Joseph, Comte de Maistre (1753-1821) who for fifteen years was a Freemason, 'nations were killed by conquest, that is by invasion: But here an important question arises; can a nation not die on its own soil, without resettlement or invasion, by allowing the flies of decomposition to corrupt to the very core those original and constituent principles which make it what it is.'

http://www.theeuroprobe.org/2012-025-the-frankfurt-school/

Parenting magazine *Baby & Family* has told readers to beware of families who are "inconspicuous" and "cheerful", as these warning signs indicate they are right wing and thus "dangerous".

Depicted with illustrations featuring solely blonde women and children, the report says ordinary parents must take action against right-wing families and make clear that their ideology has no place in the world.

http://www.breitbart.com/london/2016/09/25/blond-cheerful-families-dangerous-right/

4   The EU Coudenhove plan for mass immigration

http://www.theeuroprobe.org/2013-044-couden/

The EU want to change all the cultures of the Europeans to a single European Culture. Lenin and Stalin changed the Russian culture by starving to death millions of Kulaks. The Kulaks were small farmers and the backbone of Russian culture.

The EU are trying to do similar but by mass immigration from Africa and Middle East to ethnically dilute the White Tribes out of existence. By White tribes they mean Caucasians.

http://gatesofvienna.blogspot.co.uk/2006/10/eurabia-code_19.html

5.   From the beginning, one of the main financiers of the "Brussels EU" was the West German Government. On April 24, 1964, the key architects of the "Brussels EU" – all of them active members of the IG Farben/Nazi coalition during WWII – met at the "Brussels EU" headquarters to stake their claims on the future of the European continent. Apparently they were so sure about their success to take control over Europe in their 3rd attempt, via the "Brussels EU", that they posed proudly for this picture.

http://www.eu-facts.org/en/whoiswho/architects.html

Details the histories of the 5 1964 Committee for the German EU.

6.   The EU was set up to be initially a disguised police State. (or as Gorbachev said 'why is Europe setting itself up as a copy of the USSR?') This became more obvious (but not much) within the Maastricht Treaty. Gerard Batten, the MEP for London) has produced a very clear pamphlet showing this clearly (Appendix *6 & 66)*

7. **Must-reads** if you want to know the full extent to which the citizens of the UK have been betrayed by our political elite

Speech by Rodney Atkinson to House of Commons
https://www.youtube.com/watch?v=7Nf5KeC4dAsA

'**And into the Fire**' by Rodney Atkinson gives a far more detailed account of the EU.

'**The Great Deception**' by Booker and North. A very academic and detailed

'**The Rotten Heart of Europe**' by Bernard Connolly.

'**The Nazi Roots of the 'Brussels EU**' The Rath Foundation
Another significant book is 'The Great Deception by Booker and North. Also The Rotten Heart of Europe by Bernard Connolly
https://www.youtube.com/watch?v=7Nf5KeC4dAs

8. Most Americans have never heard of Saul Alinsky. Yet his shadow darkens our coming election. Democrat frontrunners Hillary Clinton and Barack Obama both worship at the altar of Alinskyism.
In a 1971 book called '**Rules for Radicals**', Alinsky scolded the Sixties Left for scaring off potential converts in Middle America. True revolutionaries do not flaunt their radicalism, Alinsky taught. They cut their hair, put on suits and infiltrate the system from within.

Hillary, Obama And The Cult Of Alinsky and how the Democratic Party was hijacked
http://www.theeuroprobe.org/2016-052-hillary-obama-and-the-cult-of-alinsky/

9   **EUropaische WirtschaftGemeinschaft as published in Nazi Germany in 1942 being in many ways one of the foundation documents of todays EUropean Union.**THE TRUTH WILL BE A HARD ACT TO FOLLOW for the Political scum and their apparatchiks in the EU who seek to continue to destroy Britain for their own gain in apparent compliance with this 1942 Nazi German document. I would like to thank ALL those who have given such an immense amount of help in the location, acquisition!!!, translation and now distribution

of this seminal document which undermines ALL of the LIES of ALL of the politicians about the benign and beneficial aims of the EU – they are EVIL and they are forming an Evil Union as part of the Evil concept of the New World Order comprising the vassals and their self-styled elite and their apparatchiks.

The 1942 document used as the first draft of the EU
http://www.theeuroprobe.org/2015-123-europaische-wiertschaftsgemeinschaft-the-1942-first-draft-of-the-eu/

10. A brief audit of how UK how been Asset Stripped by EU
Posted on 4 August, 2015 | 2 Comments
The 1942 German document *Europaische WirtschaftsGemeinsschaft* intended that UK would be asset stripped and all engineering and science activities which would be transferred to Germany post war.
Here's a short list of financial and industrial FUBARs from the EU
From: sounds-sensational@hotmail.co.uk
http://www.theeuroprobe.org/2015-075-an-audit-of-england-and-how-it-has-been-asset-stripped/

11 In 1944 the Germans realised they could not win the war. A meeting was held in Strasbourg to organise how to win the peace. The strategy they came up with was a bureaucratic and undemocratic society and they made preparations to set it up a post war to reassert its ambitions to rule Europe after the war *(Appendix 11))*. They would not use guns and tanks but business suits, bureaucratic procedures and the vast stocks of stolen money hidden outside of Germany.

Appendix 11 http://www.scribd.com/doc/6137969/The-Rising-Beast-Germany-in-the-Balkans

12 The 5 German leaders of the embrionic EU were all ex Nazi. From the beginning, one of the main financiers of the "Brussels EU" was the West German Government. On April 24, 1964, the key architects of the "Brussels EU" **– all of them active members of the IG Farben/Nazi coalition during WWII (IG Farben supplied the Zyklon B for the gas chambers)** – met at the "Brussels EU" headquarters to stake their claims on the future of the European continent.

(Ref 12) *http://www.theeuroprobe.org/2016-037-the-leaders-of-the-embryonic-eu/*
US Military Intelligence report EW-Pa 128

13 The Great Climate and Global Warming Fraud invented by the Club of Rome

Copies of this have been sent to several Warmists including George Monbiot at the Guardian and Dr Brian Cox at the BBC asking that if they see any inaccuracies they inform me. To date I have had not a single adverse comment. We can, therefore, assume they agree with the following and they owe me a £tenner.

The Global Warming debate can be very academic and riddled with miss understandings, half-truths and downright lies. This blog is shortened and written in non technical language for easier reading. For thoroughly researched account that gives the whole disgraceful story see The Deliberate Corruption of Climate Science by Dr Tim Ball   *http://www.theeuroprobe.org/210/*

14   In my village we had a policeman in a police house as did the next parish. He knew everyone and who the problem locals were. His children went to our village school. He also was an active participant in the village life. He was a good, honest copper.

The urban areas also had 'beat' policeman who knew their patch.

The police house was then sold and the policeman removed to car duty. This meant that the close personal contact between the policeman and the villagers was broken. The political and police authorities were clearly starting to isolate the police from the public. They were also dazzled by USA methods with officers roaring around in fast cars with 'blues and twos' as they erroneously think that such behaviour means that the public will believe they are, therefore, being very active. The BBC closed down the local friendly copper Dixon of Dock Green programme to replace it with wiz bang Z Cars to big up police in cars. Coincidence?

One of the worst things to happen to our police was the mad Macpherson Report that spuriously accused the police of 'institutional racism'. The consequence of that is they are now terrified to apply the law to 'ethnic minorities'. The Rotherham mass raping of little girls was a direct result of Macpherson as the

police allowed it rather than risk any malicious accusations of racism. The ethnic minorities and their solicitors know that and exploit it to the full.
_ *http://www.theeuroprobe.org/2013-009-whatever-has-happened-to-our-police/*

15   Agenda 21"The impulse to possess turf is a powerful one for all species; yet it is one that people must overcome. Sensitivity over the relationship between international responsibility and national sovereignty [is a]considerable obstacle to the leadership at the international level. Sovereignty is a principle which will yield only slowly and reluctantly to the imperatives of global environmental cooperation."
["Report of the Commission on Global Governance," eco-logic Magazine (publ. By Environmental Conservation Organization, Hollow Rock, TN), January/February 1996, p.4.]

Conservative environmental scientists have known for years that global forces behind the scenes were moving toward one-world government, but it was not until recently that it was possible to see the comprehensive plan, published in an official document offered to the world, entitled Our Global Neighbourhood: The Report of the Commission on Global Governance http://www.cgg.ch/CHAP1.html>. Oxford University Press
http://www.theeuroprobe.org/the-wildlands-project-to-control-all-humans-and-agenda-21/
http://www.theeuroprobe.org/2015-050-the-sinister-facts-behind-agenda-21/

http://freedomoutpost.com/george-soros-western-society-must-fall-before-one-world-govt-can-be-established/

http://www.theeuroprobe.org/2016-030-the-un-new-world-order-for-the-enslavement-of-mankind/

16   The main way that Common Purpose is subverting Britain is by infiltrating their 'graduates' into managerial positions of power in national and local government, the media, the NHS, the military, the police and the judiciary.

http://www.cpexposed.com/about-common-purpose

http://www.stopcp.com/bbcemployeescommonpurpose.php

17 Origins of the EU *http://www.theeuroprobe.org/2012-21-the-origins-of-the-eu/*

How valid is all this?
You can check for yourself. What I have done is put the evidence in a line and looked along it to see where it points.

18 Vladimer Bukovsky Russian dissident
Vladimir Bukovksy, the 63-year old former Soviet dissident, fears that the European Union is on its way to becoming another Soviet Union.
In a speech he delivered in Brussels last week Mr Bukovsky called the EU a monster that must be destroyed, the sooner the better, before it develops into a fully fledged totalitarian state.
http://www.theeuroprobe.org/2013-017-an-interview-with-soviet-dissident-vladimir-bukovsky-about-the-eussr/

19 The 1971 F&CO letter to Ted Heath stating in no uncertain terms that the then so called Common Market was, in fact, a deceitful ploy to transfer UK sovereignty to Brussels. When he said in parliament and to the British people that it was nothing more than a trading arrangement he was lying and he knew he was lying.
http://www.theeuroprobe.org/edward-heath-and-a-letter-from-the-foriegn-commonwealth-office-1972/

20 *Refs. 2014 – 021; 2014 – 014; 2015 – 050; 2015 – 033 UN Wildlands   project http://www.theeuroprobe.org/2014-021-the-wildlands-project-unleashes-its-war-on-mankind/*

21 According to a classified document, the German government now estimates that Germany will receive as many as 1.5 million asylum seekers in 2015, including 920,000 in the last quarter of 2015 alone. With family reunifications, the actual number of asylum seekers could swell to more than 7 million. Separately, German authorities now estimate that at least 290,000 migrants and refugees have entered the country without being registered.
http://www.theeuroprobe.org/2015-128-the-germany-migrant-crime-wave/

22 What will happen to the English sports teams?
Does anybody know? European National football teams, (indeed all National sports teams), are quite incompatible with the principles of the EU. The EU Toine Mander's plan is to eliminate all national teams
Will the Commission allow an 'England' sports team to exist when they have gone to such lengths to remove England from the map of Europe?
http://www.theeuroprobe.org/2013-014-what-will-happen-to-the-england-rugby-cricket-and-football-teams/

23 The EU to control all Media
http://www.theeuroprobe.org/2016-016-the-eu-to-control-all-press-and-journalists/   http://www.telegraph.co.uk/news/worldnews/13253 98/Euro-court-outlaws-criticism-of-EU. htmlhttp://www.theeuroprobe.org/2012-033-martin-tillack/

24 The organisation called the EUROGENDFOR, EGF, or more properly the European Gendarmerie Force, should be better known in Britain than it is, for its function is worrying and could affect this country in the future.
http://www.theeuroprobe.org/2013-007-eurogendfor-the-eu-paramilitary-police/

25 The Lisbon Treaty was originally the EU Constitution. This was comprehensively rejected by the French and Dutch. To get around this Giscard d'Estaing , the ex French premier, had the constitution deliberately re written in such a way that it was almost impossible for any one but a constitutional expert to understand. Several critical passages were removed and hidden in other Treaties. The label on the tin was different but the contents the same   Lisbon   http://www.theeuroprobe.org/2013-013-how-the-lisbon-treaty-was-voted-through/
http://www.theeuroprobe.org/2014-027-the-facts-about-the-lisbon-treaty/

26 The organisation called the EUROGENDFOR, EGF, or more properly the European Gendarmerie Force, should be better known in Britain than it is, for its function is worrying and could affect this country in the future.

http://www.theeuroprobe.org/2013-007-eurogendfor-the-eu-paramilitary-police/

27 http://www.theeuroprobe.org/2016-032-brexit-the-options-to-leave-the-eu/

28 Europe has had a long history of abuse of Human Rights from the Feudal System, the Spanish Inquisition, the French Revolution and the Napoleonic code to Hitler's NSDAP and Stalin's Soviet Eastern European states.
The European Court of Human Rights was started after WWII from an initiative by Eleanor Roosevelt because of the appalling abuse of Human Rights in Europe during the Nazi era. This was before the appalling behaviour of Stalin became exposed as very similar to the behaviour of the Nazi party.
http://www.theeuroprobe.org/2012-019-european-court-of-human-rights/
also European Court of Human Rights www.theeuroprobe.org 2013 – 036a

29 When he was president of the EU Romano Prodi said "there will be an EU army and only an EU army". EuroCorps intends to take over and absorb the British Armed Forces. To this end the morale, capability and facilities of our armed forces are being steadily degraded by our own political elite. It will soon be at a point where the only option left will be to hand over our hollowed out armed forces to EuroCorps as they will incapable of operating on their own.
http://www.theeuroprobe.org/2012-022-degrading-the-morale-of-uk-armed-forces/
30 This means that if you criticise to EU in the UK you can be arrested and extradited on a EAW to the EU for something that is not a crime (criticising the EU) in the UK. It is a crime in Europe Held in custody without being charged for up to 2 years and without informing your relatives where you are.We might be placated by the "double criminality rule" which basically states that the crime for which the issuing state requests extradition must also be a crime in the executing state.
http://www.theeuroprobe.org/2014-069-the-european-arrest-warrant/

http://gerardbattenmep.co.uk/2015/07/16/european-arrest-warrant-misinformation-15th-july-2015/

31   Tony Blair and Gordon Brown reneged on this promise but so has David Cameron reneged on his 'Cast Iron' promise on the feeble excuse that it is now called the 'Lisbon Treaty' instead. A recent court case challenged the decision by Gordon Brown not to have the Labour Party manifesto promise of a referendum, along with the formal statement by Tony Blair that the Labour Party manifesto was a Contract with the People. But Gordon Brown's barrister Ms. Cecelia Ivimy said on behalf of her client: "They (NuLabour manifesto promises and contracts) are not subject to legitimate expectation". Astonishing?
http://www.theeuroprobe.org/2013-020-the-value-of-party-manifestos/

32   BBC Over the last three years the BBC has secretly obtained millions of pounds in grants from the European Union. Licence fee payers might assume that the Corporation would have been compelled to disclose the source of this money in its annual reports, but they bear no trace of it specifically. In the latest set of accounts, for example, these funds are simply referred to as 'other grant income'.

http://blogs.spectator.co.uk/2014/02/the-millions-in-eu-funding-the-bbc-tried-to-hide/

33   Almost €7 billion of the EU budget was illegally spent in 2013, the European Court of Auditors (ECA) revealed on Wednesday (5 November), as it declined to sign off EU spending for the 20th consecutive year.
Although the error rate of misspent funds fell fractionally to 4.7 percent from 4.8 percent in 2012, this is still well above the 2 percent threshold under which ECA could classify payments as error-free. Spending on administration was the only part of the budget to fall within the threshold, with an estimated 1 percent error rate.
In total, EU spending in 2013 reached €148.5 billion.
https://euobserver.com/news/126405 EU Audit

34 A secret kept from the public, due to lack of media interest, is that every Government since 1972 has committed treason against the state. This ignorance has been maintained due to the media's lack of knowledge on Constitutional matters.

When Heath took the UK into the EEC, he lied to Parliament and to the British people saying that there would be no loss of sovereignty. After forty years we now know this to be untrue. This has caused a great deal of damage to the country. Sadly there are two generations of people who think this is normal. It is only people of my generation, who are in their 60's or more, who know differently.

http://www.theeuroprobe.org/?s=Edward+Heath%E2%80%99s+li es+to+the+British+Public.+Letter+from+the+Foreign+%26+Comm onwealth+Office.

35 From the beginning, one of the main financiers of the "Brussels EU" was the West German Government. On April 24, 1964, the key architects of the "Brussels EU" – all of them active members of the IG Farben/Nazi coalition during WWII – met at the "Brussels EU" headquarters to stake their claims on the future of the European continent. Apparently they were so sure about their success to take control over Europe in their 3rd attempt, via the "Brussels EU"

http://www.eu-facts.org/en/whoiswho/architects.html

36 There does seem to be some serious confusion about Vienna, Article 50 and the ECA.

This is really a subject for experts – non-experts, frankly, seem almost inevitably to fall into the trap of confusing international and domestic law, miring themselves in utter confusion in the process.
   http://www.theeuroprobe.org/2016-045-confusion-about-vienna-article-50-the-eca-and-leaving-the-eu/

37   Brexit. It is very hard for anybody not intimately involved or familiar with the EU and the workings of the UK business sector and economy to discern the nature of the advantages of Brexit. It has been made even harder by the relentless promulgation of supposed self-evident 'facts' by the government machine and its cronies. As a consequence a number of myths have begun to

crystallise around the debate which beg to be challenged and debunked. Here is a myth-busting guide addressing some of the myths and those who seek the truth about Brexit.

http://www.theeuroprobe.org/2016-014-why-its-time-to-bust-the-many-myths-surrounding-brexit/

38   BBC   The Daily Telegraph says the BBC is 'outdated' and wants it to 'demonstrate its continuing relevance'. Excuse me while I reach for my revolver. The BBC is a State broadcaster. State broadcasting was 'relevant' in the same way Communism was. Let's spell it out, for those who don't know the history. The BBC was set up to limit free speech.
 http://www.theeuroprobe.org/2015-054-the-sinister-history-of-the-bbc-form-breitbart/

39.   Tony Blair presided over a silent conspiracy to change the face of Britain for ever with mass immigration, an explosive book reveals.
He ordered his Labour government never to discuss in public the supposed 'advantages' of the unprecedented influx.
But behind the scenes ministers were instructed to wave tens of thousands of asylum seekers into the UK under cover of their being 'economic migrants'. Astonishingly, the minister Mr Blair put in charge of borders ruled against deporting failed claimants because it would be too 'emotional'.

http://www.dailymail.co.uk/news/article-3466485/How-Blair-cynically-let-two-million-migrants-Explosive-biography-reveals-PM-s-conspiracy-silence-immigration-debate.html

40.   How on earth did our MPs vote it through?
The Lisbon Treaty was originally the EU Constitution. This was comprehensively rejected by the French and Dutch. To get around this Giscard d'Estaing , the ex -French premier, had the constitution deliberately re written in such a way that it was almost impossible for anyone but a constitutional expert to understand. Several critical passages were removed and hidden in other Treaties. The label on the tin was different but the contents the same.
Gordon Brown said after he had ratified it 'I have ensured a

number of Red Lines to secure Britain's future'. Sounds good but he omitted to add that the Red Lines would be there for no more than 5 years. Was this lying? He was deceitful to such an extent that it was no different to lying.

http://www.theeuroprobe.org/2013-013-how-the-lisbon-treaty-was-voted-through/

41.   Giuliano Amato, a former prime minister of Italy, who later worked with the European Commission, helped draft the European Constitution, which became the Lisbon Treaty.
He said he had written the now infamous Article 50 but that it was largely for show.
Parliament must vote on Article 50, Dominic Grieve says
"I wrote Article 50, so I know it well," Mr Amato told a conference in Rome, according to Reuters.
He told the meeting he had specifically inserted the article to prevent the British government complaining there was no way for them to leave the bloc.

http://www.independent.co.uk/news/uk/politics/brexit-eu-referendum-britain-theresa-may-article-50-not-supposed-meant-to-be-used-trigger-giuliano-a7156656.html

42   Embarrassing   leaks   have   revealed   that   British Government officials colluded in Brussels to keep contentious issues about plans for making the EU into more of a superstate off the political agenda until after next week's referendum.
One of the most shocking of these secret proposals involves allowing 1.5 million Turks visa-free access to Britain.

http://www.dailymail.co.uk/news/article-3640078/It-s-not-just-plot-let-1-5-million-Turks-DANIEL-HANNAN-outlines-ten-bombshells-EU-s-keeping-secret-ve-voted.html

43 This article highlights the birth place of the "Brussels EU" on the drawing boards of the Nazi/IG Farben-coalition for a post-war Europe under their control. It is an excerpt of the speech by Dr. Rath on the occasion of receiving the "Relay of Life" award from survivors of the Auschwitz concentration camp.
http://www.eu-facts.org/en/background/dark_roots_europe_lecture.html

44   Common Purpose   *http://www.cpexposed.com*

45. Should it be by negotiation with the EU under Clause 50 or cut the Gordian Knot by repealing the 1972 Act?
What if we go the Lisbon Clause 50 route?
It will give the EU several years to prevaricate and keep kicking the can down the road. The EU will heavily 'bribe' the BBC, Universities, Charities, and our 'independent' national establishments to continually pester for Remain. We would also require the agreement of other EU countries who currently rely on UK continually funding them
http://www.theeuroprobe.org/2016-032-brexit-the-options-to-leave-the-eu/

46.   The State University of New York at Binghamton (SUNY-Binghamton)   is   offering   a   training   class titled "StopWhitePeople2k16," to instruct residential assistants (RAs) on how to deal with "uneducated" people who don't believe in ideas like white privilege.
The class is just one of several available to RAs at the school, and was discovered by the Binghamton Review, a student newspaper. Residential assistants are students who agree to assist with overseeing and monitoring residential life in return for receiving a free room from the school. Apparently, though, Binghamton RAs also have the responsibility of "stopping" white people.
         http://dailycaller.com/2016/08/23/taxpayer-backed-school-holds-lesson-on-how-to-stop-white-people/
47.   Clegg's fibs that the BBC allowed him to continually repeat   http://www.theeuroprobe.org/2014-066-cleggs-3-million-lost-jobs-whopper/

48   Jean-Claude Juncker's most outrageous political quotations
The former Luxembourg prime minister expected to become European Commission president tomorrow has a pragmatic approach to politics, the press and the public – and is rarely afraid to show it
http://www.telegraph.co.uk/news/worldnews/europe/eu/10967168/Jean-Claude-Junckers-most-outrageous-political-quotations.html

49.   Brussels is offering British firms cash 'bribes' of almost £1,000 a time to take on foreign workers.

Thousands of youngsters are also being offered payments totalling more than £1,100 to take a job in Britain under the European Commission scheme.

The extraordinary initiative appears to directly undermine Government efforts to persuade firms to take on British workers as the recovery takes hold

http://www.dailymail.co.uk/news/article-2379477/Brussels-offers-UK-firms-1-000-cash-bribes-hire-foreign-workers.html#ixzz4ECvuNzkf

50   New World Order (NWO) UN-Agenda-2030

The UN have unveiled their masterplan for the next 14 years – saying that they wish to implement global socialism and corporate fascism as part of their "Agenda 2030" plans. It should be remembered that the original UN Charter was written by Alger Hiss later exposed as a covert Marxist. Part of their plans, officially dubbed "Post-2015 Sustainable Development Goals," aims to reduce inequality worldwide by forcing individual governments and citizens alike to share their wealth under the guidance of a one world government.

http://www.theeuroprobe.org/2016-030-the-un-new-world-order-for-the-enslavement-of-mankind/

51   The extent of corruption in Europe is "breathtaking" and it costs the EU economy at least 120bn euros (£99bn) annually, the European Commission says.

EU Home Affairs Commissioner Cecilia Malmstroem has presented a full report on the problem. .She said the true cost of corruption was "probably much higher" than 120bn.

Three-quarters of Europeans surveyed for the Commission study said that corruption was widespread, and more than half said the level had increased.

http://www.bbc.co.uk/news/world-europe-26014387

52   "The impulse to possess turf is a powerful one for all species; yet it is one that people must overcome. sensitivity over the relationship between international responsibility and national sovereignty [is a]considerable obstacle to the leadership at the

international level. Sovereignty is a principle which will yield only slowly and reluctantly to the imperatives of global environmental cooperation."
http://www.theeuroprobe.org/the-wildlands-project-to-control-all-humans-and-agenda-21/

53 Whenever a Leftard is losing an argument they resort to accusing their opponent of being a 'Racist'. You know then they have no rational argument. What is the accusation of 'Racism'? It is a political tool used by the Frankfurt School and their followers to silence valid comments they do not wish the general public to voice or hear. It is to suppress free speech. An invention of Leon Trotsky.
It is a personal attack by the Leftards to damage your character when they cannot destroy your argument.
http://www.theeuroprobe.org/2015-009-who-originated-the-term-racist-and-why/

54 UN Agenda 21 Today, the means of pushing the New Age one-world religion is the environmental movement of the UN. The more deceptive aim of the Environmental movement, however, is its use to further the eugenics agenda, by arguing for limits to growth, and creating the backwardness that serves British Imperialism.
Its covert and fundamental aim is the eradication of the white tribes of the world.
http://www.theeuroprobe.org/2015-050-the-sinister-facts-behind-agenda-21/

55 "The impulse to possess turf is a powerful one for all species; yet it is one that people must overcome. sensitivity over the relationship between international responsibility and national sovereignty [is a]considerable obstacle to the leadership at the international level. Sovereignty is a principle which will yield only slowly and reluctantly to the imperatives of global environmental cooperation." ["Report of the Commission on Global Governance," eco-logic Magazine (publ. By Environmental Conservation Organization, Hollow Rock, TN), January/February 1996, p.4.]
http://www.theeuroprobe.org/2014-021-the-wildlands-project-unleashes-its-war-on-mankind/

56   *http://www.theeuroprobe.org/the-wildlands-project-to-control-all-humans-and-agenda-21/*

57   A historian has slammed the double standards employed in French schools which present Muslim conquerors as peaceful and brilliant, and Christians as backwards oppressors.
Against the backdrop of terror attacks and rising Islamic extremism worldwide, teacher and author Barbara Lefebvre contends that education on Islam has "never been more necessary". But the historian, who has published several books on the Holocaust, argues that textbooks' sanitisation of Muslim conquests and their presentation of an Islamic supremacist version of history is completely unhelpful.
http://www.breitbart.com/london/2016/09/30/historian-islam-demonise-christians/

58   The 1971 F&CO letter to Ted Heath stating in no uncertain terms that the then so called Common Market was, in fact, a deceitful ploy to transfer UK sovereignty to Brussels. When he said in parliament and to the British people that it was nothing more than a trading arrangement he was lying and he knew he was lying.
   http://www.theeuroprobe.org/edward-heath-and-a-letter-from-the-foriegn-commonwealth-office-1972/

59 The Nazi Roots of the Brussels EU, the key architects of the so-called 'European Union' were recruited from among the same technocrats who had previously designed the plans for a post-WW2 Europe under the control of the Nazi/IG Farben coalition. Based on literally tens of thousands of historical documents obtained by our Foundation from international archives, the growing global awareness of the facts means that the Brussels EU "experiment" is effectively now over.
   http://www.reject-the-eu.co.uk/nazi-roots/chapter.html From The Dr Rath Foundation

60   *http://www.theeuroprobe.org/2016-032-brexit-the-options-to-leave-the-eu/*

61 I decided to write this essay after a comment from a journalist, not a Leftist by my country's standards, who dismissed Eurabia

as merely a conspiracy theory, one on a par with The Protocols of the Elders of Zion. I do not disagree with the fact that conspiracy theories exist, nor that they can be dangerous. After all, the Protocols and the Dolchstosslegende, or "stab in the back myth" — the idea that Germany didn't lose WW1 but was betrayed by Socialists, intellectuals and Jews — helped pave the way for Adolf Hitler and the Nazis before WW2.
http://gatesofvienna.blogspot.co.uk/2006/10/eurabia-code_19.html

62 The bell rang three times early on a cold Friday morning before a sleepy Hans-Martin Tillack, an investigative reporter for the German newsweekly Stern, answered the door in his T-shirt and boxers. Six Belgian policemen politely filed in, he recalled, handed him a search warrant and went to work.
For the next 10 hours, they combed through his apartment and his separate office, seizing his computer hard drives, his bank records, his Filofax organizer, four cell phones, 18 boxes of files and a copy of "Spaceship Brussels," his exposé of fraud and waste inside the European Union. When Tillack complained, he recalled, one of the officers shrugged. In Burma, the policeman told him, "journalists get treated much worse."
http://www.theeuroprobe.org/2012-033-martin-tillack/

63 *_http://www.theeuroprobe.org/2015-009-who-originated-the-term-racist-and-why/*

64 In a crass and ill-timed intervention, the unelected president of the European Council Herman Van Rompuy has warned Vladimir Putin that the EU intends ultimately to control every country on the western flank of Russia.
In an interview with *De Standaard* newspaper, Van Rompuy speaks about his "dreams" that all the Balkan states will join the EU. He calls it an "inspiring thought" that in the long term "the whole of European territory outside Russia" will be tied to the EU http://www.breitbart.com/london/2014/05/01/van-rompuy-says-europe-will-expand-without-public-backing/

65 *BBC Newsnight – Comments*
https://m.facebook.com/bbcnews/posts/10153401828537217
BBC to be impartial? However it has been overtly and subliminally

backing the "stay in" on the grounds that "the *British* people are *too stupid to understand what the EU is about.* https://www.google.co.uk/webhp?sourceid=chrome-instant&ion=1&espv=2&ie=UTF-8#q=BBC+Newsnight+British+too+stupid+to+govern+themselves

66 By Gerard Batten MEP who is perhaps the most clued MEP on this subject http://gerardbattenmep.co.uk/2015/04/13/eu-police-states-comes-one-stop-closer/

67 http://www.stopcp.com/bbcemployeescommonpurpose.php

68 *http://www.dailymail.co.uk/news/article-1179902/Revealed-The-secret-report-shows-Nazis-planned-Fourth-Reich--EU.html*

69 Jack Straw *http://www.azquotes.com/quote/705883* Peter Sutherland *http://www.azquotes.com/quote/705883*

70 List of BBC staff who are Common Purpose alumni http://www.stopcp.com/bbcemployeescommonpurpose.php

71 *Mitterands quote to destroy England by linking it with Europe http://www.mirror.co.uk/news/uk-news/thatcher-in-threat-nuke-argies-572432*

72 *http://www.theeuroprobe.org/2012-051-transatlantic-trade-and-investment-partnership-ttpi/*

73 *http://www.mirror.co.uk/news/uk-news/thatcher-in-threat-nuke-argies-572432*

74 http://www.dailymail.co.uk/news/article-2379477/Brussels-offers-UK-firms-1-000-cash-bribes-hire-foreign-workers.html#ixzz4ECvuNzkf

75 http://www.breitbart.com/london/2016/10/15/mps-lodge-protest-bbc-new-research-confirms-anti-brexit-bias/

76 Corruption in the http://www.bbc.co.uk/news/world-europe-26014387

77   http://www.theeuroprobe.org/the-wildlands-project-to-control-all-humans-and-agenda-21/
http://www.theeuroprobe.org/2016-030-the-un-new-world-order-for-the-enslavement-of-mankind/
http://www.theeuroprobe.org/2014-021-the-wildlands-project-unleashes-its-war-on-mankind/http://www.theeuroprobe.org/2014-021-the-wildlands-project-unleashes-its-war-on-mankind/

78   https://wattsupwiththat.com/2016/10/22/a-review-of-25-myths-that-are-destroying-the-environment/

INDEX